INDIAN MUSALMANS

INDIAN MUSALMANS:

BEING

THREE LETTERS

W. NASSAU LEES.

GYAN

Published by

Gyan Publishing House
5, Ansari Road
Daryaganj, New Delhi-110002
Phone: 011-47034999, 9811692060
E-mail: books@gyanbooks.com

Distribution Network
gyanbooks.com
India, USA, Canada, UK, Australia, France

ISBN : 978-81-212-9562-8 (PB)
First Published, 1871

2nd Impression 2023

Printed at: Gyan Press, Delhi.

INDIAN MUSALMANS
Author: W. NASSAU LEES.

INDIAN MUSALMÁNS:

BEING

THREE LETTERS

REPRINTED FROM THE "TIMES,"

WITH AN

Article on the late Prince Consort,

AND

FOUR ARTICLES ON EDUCATION,

REPRINTED FROM THE "CALCUTTA ENGLISHMAN."

WITH AN APPENDIX

CONTAINING

LORD MACAULAY'S MINUTE.

BY

W. NASSAU LEES,

FELLOW OF THE CALCUTTA UNIVERSITY; DOCTOR OF LAWS OF DUBLIN UNIVERSITY; DOCTOR OF PHILOSOPHY OF THE BERLIN UNIVERSITY; LATE PRINCIPAL OF THE MOHAMMADAN COLLEGE OF CALCUTTA, ETC.

1871.

ADVERTISEMENT.

There has long been a misconception regarding my views on Education in India, and as that misconception seems to have extended to this country, I publish in connection with the three letters on Indian Musalmáns, I have lately addressed to the *Times* some extracts from a series of articles I wrote in 1866 in the Calcutta *Englishman*. Because I deplore the neglect of the Oriental classical languages in the Government system of Education in India, many come to the conclusion that I wish to revive the early policy of the East India Company of subsidizing exclusively the study of these languages to the exclusion of English, and some go so far as to assert that my object is to revert to the policy of Warren Hastings, and keep the Civil Administration of British India in the hands of the Musalmáns. I have so repeatedly denied these assertions, that it seems useless for me to do so any more. I will, therefore, only add that my conviction is so firm that any attempts to denationalize the people of India by denying the higher classes access to their own classics, and teaching them only English, will so utterly fail, that sooner or later the attempt will be given up. Then possibly a system of Public Instruction for the people, having better claims to be called National than the present, may be devised, in which English, Sanskrit, Arabic, Persian, and the Vernaculars will all be found in their proper places, no undue favour being shewn to the study of any.

Judging from Lord Mayo's recent excellent Resolution on this subject, his Lordship seems to have become alive to the fact that the existing system is not quite what it ought to be—the first step towards a reform; and as His Excellency's Resolution goes some way to establish my own position, I reprint it *in extenso* :—

"*Extract from the Proceedings of the Government of India in the Home Department* (*Education*)." — SIMLA, *August*, 1871.

RESOLUTION.

THE condition of the Mohammadan population of India as regards education, has of late been frequently pressed upon the attention of the Government of India from statistics recently submitted to the Governor-General in Council. It is evident that in no part of the country except, perhaps, the North-Western Provinces and the Punjab, do the Mohammadans adequately or in proportion to the rest of the community avail themselves of the educational advantages that the Government offers. It is much to be regretted that so large and important a class, having a classical literature replete with works of profound learning and great value, and counting among them a section specially devoted to the acquisition and diffusion of knowledge, should stand aloof from active co-operation with our educational system, and should lose the advantages, both material and social, which others enjoy. His Excellency in Council believes that secondary and higher education conveyed in the vernaculars and rendered more accessible than now, coupled with a more systematic encouragement and recognition of Arabic and Persian literature, would be not only acceptable to the Mohammadan community but would enlist the sympathies of the more earnest and enlightened of its members on the side of education.

2. The Governor-General in Council is desirous that further encouragement should be given to the classical and vernacular languages of the Mohammadans in all Government schools and colleges. This need not involve any alterations in the subjects, but only in the media of instruction. In avowedly English schools established in Mohammadan districts, the appointment of qualified Mohammadan English teachers might, with advantage, be encouraged. As in vernacular schools, so in this class also, assistance might justly be given to Mohammadans by grants-in-aid to create schools of their own. Greater encouragement should also be given to the creation of a vernacular literature for the Mohammadans, a measure the importance of which was specially urged upon the Government of India by Her Majesty's Secretary of State on more than one occasion.

3. His Excellency in Council desires to call the attention of local Governments and Administrations to this subject, and directs that this Resolution be communicated to them, and to the Universities in India, with a view of eliciting their opinions whether, without infringing the fundamental principles of our educational system, some general measure in regard to Mohammadan education

might not be adopted, and whether more encouragement might not be given in the University course to Arabic and Persian literature. The authorities of the Lahore University College, who are believed to have paid much attention to the subject, should also be invited to offer their views on the important question above referred to. This may be done through the Punjab Government.

The only objection I have to make to this Resolution is that it proposes to legislate for the better education of the Musalmán population of India only, whereas it is time, in my humble judgment, to consider the question of the Education of the Musalmáns as a part of the greater question—the Education of the people of India as that congeries of Nationalities called Her Majesty's Indian Empire.

Athenæum, Nov. 10, 1871.

INDIAN MUSALMÁNS.

To the Editor of the Times.

Oct. 14, 1871.

SIR,

ABSENCE in the Highlands has prevented me from sooner noticing the letters which have appeared in your columns regarding the assassination of the late lamented Mr. Justice Norman. I knew him well, and I can add my testimony to that of the many who have given public expression to the feelings of deep regret which they entertain for his loss, to the kind and benevolent character of his nature, and to the sincere interest he took in the welfare of the natives of India, and especially that of the Mohammadan community of Calcutta. I feel the most confident conviction, then, that it is next to a moral impossibility the foul deed which has just been perpetrated could have had its origin in any feelings of animosity or even personal dislike to one who was all that "Amicus Mœrens" and the "Head Master of Wicksworth Grammar School" stated him to have been, and that, consequently, Mr. Justice Norman owes his death to the unflinching integrity with which he discharged the public duties of his office.

I wish I could close my letter with this brief testimonial to the worth of the excellent and humane Judge who has just fallen by the dagger of the assassin; but there is a political question of such very grave importance raised in the correspondence under notice, regarding which, looking to the relationship in which I have stood to the educated Mohammadans of Bengal for the past twelve or fourteen years, I feel it my duty to them, as well as to the Government which I have the honour to serve, to do my best to aid the public in coming to a right conclusion.

I allude to the charges of disloyalty to the Queen which this melancholy event has called forth from correspondents in your columns against Her Majesty's Indian Mohammadan subjects—charges made general rather by implication than by direct statements. These charges have been indignantly repelled, I am glad to observe, by "A Mahomedan" in his letter of the 27th ult., published in your issue of the day following. I not only firmly believe in the sincerity of the professions of loyalty and fidelity to which this writer has given utterance, but I desire to add my concurrence in his sentiments so far as they affect the great body of his co-religionists in India, who, I am quite certain, will repudiate with indignation and horror the crime which has been committed by one of their body.

At the same time, while I cordially endorse the

opinion expressed by "A Mahomedan," that the crimes and follies of a few misguided men or a small section of the Indian Mohammadans "should not bring into odium or cast discredit on the Musalmán population at large," I think that if he is well informed as to the feelings and political opinions of his co-religionists in India—and though a Musalmán, it is quite possible that he may not be—it is inconsistent with that loyalty which he professes, and which, as I said, I have not the slightest doubt that he sincerely feels, to deny that the discontent, dissatisfaction, hostility, or whatever you please to call it, which a certain proportion of Her Majesty's Musalmán subjects not only feel but show to British rule in India is, as "A Civilian" says, "a constant source of anxiety" and a "difficulty" to the Government of India. Whether, moreover, this proportion be large or small, it is idle to assert that it is "composed of the veriest dregs of society, with no position whatever except among their own set," as long as indisputable evidence is forthcoming to show that it was instrumental in intensifying the hostile and bitter feelings of fourteen years ago, and fomenting and fostering, if it did not originate the Mutiny or Rebellion of 1857-58; that it had sufficient strength to aid materially in keeping our North-western frontier in a state of chronic warfare for years, involving the despatch of eighteen or twenty military expeditions, aggregating some 30,000 or 40,000 men across the Indus; that, in spite of the severest chastisement, it had the daring six or seven years after the wholesale massacres of 1857-58, to hatch a conspiracy in the very heart of Bengal proper, which composed a hostile demonstration against us of such magnitude that it cost the loss of nearly 1000 British soldiers and 50 officers; that it has had for the last forty years, and still has influence within India, to place under contribution or black mail a very large proportion indeed of that loyal and highly respectable section of the community to which "A Mahomedan" probably belongs, for purposes which are in no way conducive to the interests of British rule in India, or British interests in the East; and that in all probability it is to the influence of this section of the community we owe the assassination of the officiating Chief Justice Norman, of Her Majesty's High Court of Justice.

If I may be allowed to mediate between the two classes of your correspondents—the Christian and the Moslim—I would say that the Indian Government has not only very good and sound cause for any anxiety it may feel on this important subject, but it would, in my humble judgment, be far better both for India and for the Mohammadan community at large, if that anxiety had very long ago shewn itself in a more practical form, and were now very much greater than it is.

There are two issues, moreover, involved in this momentous question—viz., disloyalty to the Sovereign; and dissatisfaction with British rule, which, although they cannot be entirely dissociated, ought not to be indiscriminately mixed up together. It has often before been argued, and is often now discussed, whether loyalty to a Christian Sovereign is compatible with a strict observance of the Canonical Law. On this point, however, I do not think much writing is needed. Mohammadan Law, similarly with the laws of the Medes and Persians, is not changed by Act of Parliament. It is the same to-day, in the letter, as when Khálid ibn al-Walíd (the Sword of God) conquered Syria, and 'Amr ibn al-Aás Egypt. Acceptance of the Faith, the payment of Tribute, or the Sword, are the terms it offers to unbelievers —when *Islám* is in the ascendant. When it is not, the Faithful are *majbúr* or helpless, and incur no moral responsibility by submitting to the yoke of the conqueror; nor, having done so, are they under any obligation of conscience to rise in rebellion and throw it off, nor, under certain conditions, to migrate. The waning influence, moreover, of the temporal power of Mohammadanism has caused Mohammadan Doctors of Theology to interpret the law in a light very favourable to the peace of mind of Indian Moslims. I discussed this point at length at Cairo in 1858 with Al-Bagúri, the then venerable Shaikh al-Islám of Egypt, I arguing for the affirmative, and he for the negative of the proposition; but neither of us got very far beyond the texts, "Kill them wheresoever ye find them," and

" Ye are in no wise bound to rush upon your own destruction." (I have no Koran at hand to give chapter and verse.) The inference to be drawn from the Shaikh's arguments, whether based on the Koran or the Canons, and which I believe to be the accepted rule, is that under a strong, just, and liberal Christian Government—*i.e.*, a Government under which perfect civil and religious freedom is allowed—a Mohammadan may be as true and loyal to his Sovereign, though a Christian, as any of his Christian subjects, and not infringe the Law; although should the Government be weak, he would be bound to aid any Mohammadan movement which he had sound reason to believe was sufficiently powerful to overthrow the existing Government, and set up a Mohammadan Government in its stead. Should it be strong and oppressive, it would then be his duty to leave the country. And that this doctrine, I may add, although not having the force of Law, would be the rule and practice with Christians or the followers of any religion under the sun, who should find themselves under the Government of an alien race, we have had abundant proof in Europe.

This is the Law. But there are sects in India, as there are in other parts of the East, who do not recognize the doctrines or the law of the orthodox Moslim; and who, even under Mohammadan Governments, would give endless trouble if not kept in order. Abd-al-Wahháb, who rose in rebellion against the Sultan, overran Arabia, sacked Mecca, deluged the country with blood, and gave so much trouble to the Porte about 140 years ago, was the founder of one of them. He was a reformer, and the peculiar tenets of his belief were brought to India and propagated by the well-known Saiyid Ahmad and his disciples some forty years ago or more; and since then, what with Moplahs, Firázis, Titu Miyans, and those now known under the general name of Wahhábis (most of whom, be it remarked, flourish in Bengal Proper), there has been a good deal of trouble and loss of life, and an enormous expenditure of public money. Few people know much, if anything, of these things in England, nor, for that matter, in India either. I know of no one here who is well acquainted with the history of Mohammadan risings and disturbances in Bengal, unless it be Sir Frederick Halliday, formerly Lieutenant-Governor of that Province, and now a member of the Council of Her Majesty's Secretary of State for India. It is for that reason I have thought it well to address you, for it ought not to be concealed, but, on the contrary, it ought to be clearly and publicly made known that if, as there is too much reason to believe, the murderer of Mr. Justice Norman was a hired assassin, he was certainly not hired to do this deed by any association composed of the "dregs of society," but by a body of considerable political power, and of so much daring that, had it suited their purpose, Her Majesty's Viceroy, instead of her Chief Justice, would have been the victim singled out for destruction. If we have in the heart of our Indian Empire, or scattered throughout our territories, those who are an anxiety to Government and a danger to our rule, it is much better that the source of that anxiety and the cause of it should be acknowledged; and that people who do not understand the subject, or who have no means of ascertaining the truth, should not confound the whole of Her Majesty's Indian Mohammadan subjects with a small minority of malcontents.

We cannot suppress freedom of thought or conscience in India any more than we can in Ireland. Still less can we propose to exterminate large bodies of people, even though their religious or political opinions are dangerous to the peace of our Empire. They will exist in the East as they do in the West. It is gratifying, however, to feel assured that in India they form but a small proportion of the 20,000,000 of Her Majesty's Mohammadan subjects, and that as long as the great body of Mohammadans are satisfied, and live contentedly under British rule, it is within the power of the Indian Government to reduce the danger alluded to to a *minimum*.

This brings me to the second point in the inquiry; but already I have trespassed too much on your space, and must defer it to another occasion, if you think the subject of sufficient public importance to admit this long letter to a place in your columns.

October 20, 1871.

SIR,—In concluding my letter upon Indian Musalmáns which you did me the honour to publish in *The Times* of the 14th inst., I said it was within the power of the British Government to reduce the danger from Musalmán malcontents to a a *minimum*. Many people are of opinion that the Musalmáns are quite prepared to accept the supremacy of the English as an evil which must be endured because it cannot be cured. I go further. I believe that they are quite prepared to live as peaceably and contentedly under British rule as they would under any Mohammadan Government they are likely to see established on its ruins, provided they are considerately treated and wisely and well governed. And I am justified in saying so much, for, were it otherwise, large numbers of the nomadic Musalmán population of British India would be found continually streaming into the territories of the Nazim of Hyderabad, and other Musalmán native States, as well as crossing the frontiers into Afghanistan, which we do not find to be the case.

The question, then, from this point of view, is, are Indian Musalmáns considerately treated and well and wisely governed. Nor will it be a sufficient answer to this question on the part of the British Government to say that it is enough that the Musalmáns prefer it to the rule of the native Mohammadan princes within and beyond our frontiers. It is one of the misfortunes of our position in India that, affecting a moral superiority over the races we govern, we at once institute a comparison, and invite our subjects to try us by a very much higher standard than could fairly be applied to a native Government. To deny this, moreover, would be to abandon the proud position we make it our boast to occupy, as regenerators of a fourth of the human race.

Since I last addressed you I have seen Dr. W. W. Hunter's remarkable work upon Indian Musalmáns, to which you have alluded. I desire to speak in terms of high commendation of a work so eminently calculated to draw the attention of the public to a subject of very grave importance to the welfare and peace of British India—one which has been too long neglected, although I think it unfortunate that this able and intelligent writer, to accomplish his aim, has been under the necessity of giving a somewhat too sensational character to his otherwise extremely interesting and valuable work. It is, perhaps, to be regretted, too, that Mr. Hunter has thought it advisable to criticize, and thus, in a measure, discredit the decisions of the highest authorities in India and Arabia upon points of Law upon which, whatever their secret opinions be, it may be assumed their special knowledge is more profound than that of any European in India. It is not my intention to enter into this subject; but I may observe, *en passant*, that the *Usúl ud-din*, or the principles of the Moslim faith, according to the *Sunnis*, are four—the *Kurán*, or Holy Word of God; the *Hadíth*, or decisions of the Prophet, which were collected in large volumes by Al-Bokhári, Al-Muslim, and four others, constituting the Canons of Islam; the *Ijmâi Aiyumma*, or concurrence of the Doctors; and *Kiyàs*, or intelligent interpretation. There is little use, in theological discussions, in appealing to the bald texts of either the *Kurán* or the Canons. As you rightly observe, in your very able and sound article of the 14th inst., the Law, as to be derived from these sources, was framed for a conquering and not for a subject race. Texts, such as the forty *Hadíth*, on Holy War, could be culled from them to prove anything but what would be conducive to the interests of the Musalmáns at large. They themselves early discovered this, and hence the authoritative decisions of the *Shaikh-ul-Islám*, and other competent authorities, are invested with very great weight in Mohammadan countries.

From this point of view, the *futwahs* lately given by the Muftis of Mecca and by the learned Musalmáns of Delhi, Lucknow, and Rampoor, in favour of India being *dár ul-Islám*, or a country in which

Moslims may reside, are, or ought to be, of singular importance to the Government of India and its Musalmán subjects. For this reason I am sorry to find my friend Mr. Hunter, who deserves so well of Indian Musalmáns, outheroding Herod, if I may use the expression of one who, judging him by his own evidence, would be a Wahhábi, if he were not too good a Sunni or Shiah Moslim. If the Government of India have shewn a want of political sagacity in one respect more than another in their treatment of the Wahhábi difficulty, it is in not having taken greater pains to place the large body of their well-affected Musalmán subjects in a better position to resist the attacks upon their loyalty or any attempts to undermine it, on the score of religion, than they now are, to protect them, as it were, from incurring the *odium theologicum*. This the present Government of India is, I believe, very well aware of.

I do not in any wise mean to assert that the Government of India, continuing to pursue the policy of Warren Hastings, should have kept the civil administration of the country in the hands of the Musalmáns, or have adopted all or any of the early traditions of the East India Company; nor that it should have secured to the Musalmáns, in consideration of their 600 years of conquering supremacy, any special privileges, civil or religious, over Hindoos or Christians; nor yet that out of deference to their unwillingness to accommodate themselves to the altered circumstances of their position —their stiff-neckedness—the progress of the country should have been arrested one hour. Still having come into possession—how, it is of no moment to inquire—of a Musalmán inheritance of many centuries' date, more care, I think might have been taken to insure, as far as in us lay, that if comparisons between past and present were made, they should be as much as possible in our favour. Starting from our own stand-point of strictly religious neutrality, both Hindoos and Mohammadans might reasonably object to a considerable sum out of the revenues raised by the sweat of their brows being devoted annually to the maintenance of an Established Church for the benefit of Christians, be they Government servants or not, while no annual grant at all from the revenues is made for the support of Hindoo and Mohammadan places of worship, or for their clergy. The natives of India, as far as I am aware, have never taken objection to this grant. With the Musalmáns possibly our position would not be improved were it discontinued, for then from *Ahl i Kitáb*, or people of the Book (Holy Scriptures), we might come into the category of infidels. I mention the fact, then, not disapprovingly, but rather to give point to the complaints of the Musalmáns, which I believe to be as under:—

They object (1) that the Inám Commission unjustly deprived many of their class of the lands granted to them by the Mohammadan Sovereigns of India; that (2) their civil and religious law, which Her Majesty had bound herself never to interfere with, has been broken by the Act securing to converts to Christianity the rights of inheritance, which they had forfeited under the Mohammadan code, and that thus the British Government, while offering inducements to conversion to Christianity, has weakened the foundations of Islám; that (3) the appointment of Kádhi (Cazi) and Government Mohammadán law officers has been abolished, whereby they have been deprived of the benefit of properly constituted authorities to perform and register many of their civil rites; that (4) funds left by charitable and pious Moslims for educational purposes have been taken from them, and religious bequests *(wakf)*, or funds left to be devoted to the "service of God," have been misapplied by Government, which is the self-appointed trustee for their proper administration; that (5) they have been elbowed out of almost all Government appointments by Hindoos, and no efforts are made by Government to rectify this injustice or to better their prospects; that (6) no offices under Government are open to Musalmáns learned in their own sciences, laws, literature, and languages; that consequently learning and learned men have disappeared, and their community is left in darkness, while the Government system of education is such that they cannot accept it and retain the respect of their co-religionists, if even they may remain good Moslims.

The above, which I believe to be the main grievances put forward by Indian Musalmáns—chiefly in Bengal, be it observed—I have stated exactly as they have often been represented to me. They have others, which in secret they brood over, but it is unnecessary to allude to them, as they are inevitable under British rule, and irremediable unless under a dynastic change. I have no desire to endorse all these complaints, although I think many of them are well founded, and in all of them I sympathize with the Musalmáns of India, who, from being the proud rulers of the Indian Empire, I find now in danger of being reduced to the level of hewers of wood and drawers of water unless something is done for them. It would not be for the honour and glory of England that history should record the consummation of such a result; while it will certainly not be for the interest of the British Government that, as some of its counsellors advise, it should aid in bringing it about.

Some are of opinion that all the Musalmáns' complaints are based upon hatred of the Christian. It is certainly not so. They have infinitely more reason on their side than those who do not understand them are aware of. Many high Indian officials have gone beyond the Musalmáns in admitting that (1) some of the proceedings of the Inám Commission were "iniquitous." In regard again (2) to the Act securing the rights of inheritance to Christian converts, however just in the abstract, it was in statecraft a blunder, because in reference to Mohammadans it was uncalled for, converts from that religion being almost unknown. It was passed at the instance of the missionaries, and was calculated to attain a *minimum* of good with a very large result of political evil. Touching the abolition of (3) the Kádhi al-Kudhát, or Chief Justice, and other Khádhis, again, the same or similar remarks will apply. They were no expense to Government, and, although they had no administrative functions, their existence furnished all well-disposed Musalmáns with an argument of some weight against their co-religionists who asserted that India was no longer *dár ul-Islám.* After the terrible scenes of 1857-58 this view was very generally maintained, and numbers of Musalmáns in consequence left India and went to reside at Mecca, Medinah, Kurballah, and other places in Arabia. The objections to the measure were at my instance laid before the Governor-General by Sir H. Harington, who has just been laid in his grave; but there being no Kádhis in the Punjab it was thought they could be dispensed with in Bengal. The Government of India, in the application of the Marriage Registration Act, have since discovered that this was a mistake. That (4) educational funds and *wakf* bequests have been misappropriated is well known to many persons even in England. When in India for a brief period in 1869-70 I was informed that a resolution was about to issue from the Government of India acknowledging the fact, and instituting an inquiry with a view to restitution; but no such resolution that I am aware of has yet, I regret to say, been published. Yet I have heard Moslims stigmatize the misappropriation of trust funds left by Muhammad Mohsin (the Hooghly Madrassah) as a State robbery, and I do not hesitate to say that it was not creditable to British rule. The objections of the Musalmáns to the educational system of the Government of India, and their ceasing to obtain a fair share of Government appointments are in my humble judgment of grave importance; but the subject is too large to be treated of at the tail end of a long letter.

The redress of the grievances of the Musalmáns of India is a question of great difficulty. That is a good reason, you will say, for the Government no longer evading its consideration ; but there is possibly a still better one, one which the Musalmáns have not had the acumen to detect the full force of, viz. that the discontented feeling which exists among the Mohammadans of Bengal is more the fault of Government than of the Musalmáns, for in Bengal certainly it is due mainly to those unjust and iniquitous proceedings of early Indian Governments which made landlords out of Hindú collectors of revenue, and finally crystallized the injustice thus done to the community in general, and the Mohammadan portion of it in particular, by that gigantic blunder, the Perpetual Settlement, which having necessitated the Income-Tax and other measures of direct taxation, has brought odium upon the Government, and placed the whole of India under unequal and unjust contribution.

November 2, 1871.

Sir,—In my first letter upon Indian Musalmáns, I addressed myself to their loyalty to their Sovereign, Queen Victoria ; in my second I discussed their alleged discontent with British rule ; and in this letter I propose, with your permission, to say a word upon the redress of their grievances in so far as that is possible under the government of an alien race.

It would not, certainly, be easy now to redress the injustice done by the resumption of rent-free tenures under the operation of the Inám Commission. But there would be no difficulty in repealing the Act interfering with the laws of inheritance as regards Moslims, or the Act II., of 1864 in so far as it relates to the Kádhi-al-Kudhát, or the local Kádhis. Still less difficulty would there be in restoring to the Musalmáns, with simple interest, and after an accurate account had been taken, all *wakf* bequests and educational funds left for their exclusive benefit.

Still, all this, though it would go a considerable

way to satisfy the minds of Indian Musalmáns that there was no intention on the part of the British Government to look upon them with disfavour or to depress them, would go but a small way towards compassing that moral and intellectual regeneration of the race which would raise them in the social scale and secure for them that ease of circumstances which begets contentment,—another term for loyalty to the ruling power. Measures wider in their scope, more permeating in their influence, and more lasting in their results are necessary, and you, Sir, in your able article of the 14th inst., have indicated the direction they should take. They are, primarily, such a modification of the Government educational system as will induce the Musalmáns of India, in common with all other races and creeds, to avail themselves of its benefits, and such a reform of Musalmán collegiate institutions as I have myself many years ago advocated.

A prosperous people are usually satisfied with their Government; a poverty-stricken people are invariably discontented with it. But for a people to be prosperous it is necessary that they should be actively employed; to be actively employed they must be fitted for employment; and to be fitted for employment they must be instructed, if not educated. The logic of this simple syllogism I take to be indisputable. The means, however, employed to accomplish this end, to be effectual, must not be those simply which a Government, in its wisdom, approves, and strives capriciously or conscientiously to adopt ; they must be those which the people for whose benefit they are intended can, or at least will, consent to accept. All may not so readily assent to this latter proposition, but at the present hour, with the results of the blundering policy which for years has been adopted with reference to Ireland staring us in the face, it would, in my humble judgment, be childish to waste time in discussing either it or the converse of it. I will pass on then to review the question more in detail, but in doing so it will be desirable to clear the ground by taking a brief retrospect of what has been done by the Government of India for the past century of British rule in India.

In the earlier years of the occupation of India by the English almost the whole of the time and thoughts of the Indian Government were taken up with measures of conquest. The natural result was that the civil government of the country—always excepting the collection of revenue—was neglected, and the social institutions which existed under the old *régime* became so dislocated that Government soon found itself embarrassed for properly qualified officers to discharge the duties of the judicial and revenue departments of the State. This state of things induced that great statesman, Warren Hastings, to record a Minute in which he declared that learning was disappearing from the land, and that, as the Government considered it expedient to retain the civil administration of the country in the hands of the Musalmáns, an institution for their education should be established. With this view he laid the foundation of the present Mohammadan College of Calcutta. At first Warren Hastings maintained the institution entirely at his own cost; but finally his measures were approved and sanctioned by the Court of Directors, who endowed this college with a grant of land then yielding 32,000 rupees (£3,200) a year. This grant by the Government of Sir John Shore (Lord Teignmouth) was afterwards ordered to be separated from the general revenues of the State for the benefit of the institution. Subsequently the Court of Directors sanctioned an annual grant of £10,000 a year for the purposes of education throughout their territories. The policy then adopted supplied the Government with a sufficient number of Musalmán civil officers for all its purposes. The Mohammadan College of Calcutta was, in fact, the Haileybury of Bengal. But the grant was, of course, utterly ineffectual as a means of educating the people. Yet was the early policy of the Court of Directors not wholly inoperative, or without some good results. The encouragement given by the Government to the study of the Laws, Literature, and Languages of the natives gave birth to a small band of Englishmen distinguished as statesmen, lawgivers, and scholars, whose names will live in the memory of the people of India as long as, and perhaps longer than, our Government lasts. I need only mention the names of Sir William Jones, Colebrooke, Macnaghten, James Prinsep, Horace Wilson, John Gilchrist, &c., to prove that however unsuitable to the present day, the policy of the then Home and Indian Governments was not altogether a mistake. Things ran on in this groove for thirty or forty years, at the close of which there was plenty of learning, and no lack of learned men, as those terms are understood in the East, in Bengal. Governors and governed seemed satisfied with each other. But a reformer was born in the person of Thomas Babington, Lord Macaulay, who rudely broke the spell of the enchanted circle. He declared that the books of the Hindoos contained nothing but mythological fables and absurd superstition, and those of the Musalmáns nothing but false science, false philosophy, and false religion. The English language, he averred, was the "key of knowledge," and for the ruling power to withhold it from the conquered natives was to deny them the means of elevating themselves in the social scale to a level with their European conquerors. A hotly and well-maintained struggle between the advocates of the old and the proposed new system ensued, in which the best intellects in India took part. This contest was known as the "Battle of the Orientalists and the Anglicists," and ended in the discomfiture of the former, and the victory and triumph of the latter, or the party of Macaulay. From that day English has been recognised as the medium of higher education in India, and the subjects taught in it have been entirely European. Still the change then effected amounted, as regards the education of the people, to nothing ; and, as regards the upper classes in Bengal, ostensibly to little more than the substitution of the Hindu College, with an English education for Hindus, for the Mohammadan College, with a Musalmán education for the followers of Islam, for no funds were made available for educational measures on an extended scale. Virtually, however, the change made was of considerable political importance, for its effect was the gradual but steady transfer of the civil government of the country from the Musalmáns to the Hindús, without any authoritative enunciation of the change in the policy of the British Government in this respect, nor the introduction of any statesmanlike measure that would obviate evil results. Ousted from their rights in the soil by the perpetual settlement of Lord Cornwallis, it is only very recently, indeed, that the Musalmáns of Bengal have awoke to the discovery that by the change in the educational policy of the Government of India made thirty-five years ago they have been ousted out of not simply their monopoly, but even a fair share of Government patronage.

About twenty years later (1854) Lord Halifax, through the first Educational Despatch worthy of the name issued by the British Government, (it nominally issued from the Court of Directors), constituted an Educational Department for all India, and provided funds from the revenues of the country for maintaining it. By this despatch the Government founded the Universities of Calcutta, Madras, and Bombay, connecting with them by a system of link Scholarships all the institutions in the country for the general education of the people, from the highest collegiate institution to the lowest vernacular school, and prescribed English for higher and middle, and the vernacular for lower education, as *media* for instruction. No provision was made in the general scheme then promulgated for the classical languages of India—Sanskrit and Arabic—English and the vernaculars taking their place; nor in carrying out the measure was any place in the system accorded to the Mohammadan College of Calcutta, the Sanskrit Colleges of Calcutta or Benares, nor to other so-called Oriental Colleges in which these languages were taught, though they were directed to be maintained.

The Education Despatch of 1854 was replete with confessions as to the shortcomings of the British Government in regard to measures for the education of the people, and rife with promises of future improvement. It contained many noble and lofty sentiments, and was in all respects highly honourable to its framers and the Government that issued it. It had, however, serious defects. All new measures of the kind have and must have defects, which their practical working alone can disclose, and the Home Government of India did not assume for their great and good measure a perfection unattainable in human affairs. The Government of India was called upon for a report upon the measure by Lord Stanley when he was Secretary of State for India in 1859, or within five years after it came into operation. Information was collected in India, but no report was furnished. Some years later Sir Stafford Northcote again called for a report. The same process was gone through in India with not quite, but very nearly the same results. Notes and memoranda there have been, but no comprehensive report by the Government of India to the Secretary of State upon the working of, and the results of the Education Despatches of 1854 and 1859 has yet been written or published. And yet the policy therein laid down has been so far departed from in the Bengal Presidency that the classical languages were put in place of the vernaculars in higher education without the sanction of the Secretary of State in Council, and without the knowledge even of the Government of India. True an alteration in the Regulations of the Calcutta University was reported to Government by the Syndicate, but in such a manner as to lead Government to believe that the proposed change was of the most insignificant importance. And it is in defence of the Government of India I make this statement, for the change brought the whole fabric of Lord Halifax's despatch of 1854, which was based on affiliated Anglo-vernacular colleges and middle-class and vernacular schools, connected by a system of link Scholarships, to the ground, threw the Calcutta University out of sympathy with the sister Universities of Madras and Bombay, and involved the entire Department of Education in Bengal in inexplicable confusion. Nor was it till the change was completed that its mischievous effects were discovered, and the sole plan for remedying the evils which suggested itself to the educational authorities in Bengal was the destruction of the Mohammadan College of Calcutta and other Oriental colleges in Bengal, or their absorption into the Presidency English College, or into the general system, which means the same thing.

No blame, then, can attach to the Secretary of State for India, if now, after the lapse of nearly twenty years, he is unable to inform Parliament if the noble scheme for the education of the people of India, inaugurated in 1854, is suitable for them, or whether all classes of Her Majesty's Indian subjects equally avail themselves of its benefits, for though a mass of voluminous documents and returns are periodically printed and sent home, no despatch from the Government of India upon the whole question has reached the India Office. Nor am I surprised that the Government of India should shrink from the responsibility of the task, from a sense of inability to dictate any despatch that would not be more misleading in its conclusions than likely to furnish sound *data* for future legislation. One of the most mischievous effects of the new system was that it enabled the Government of India to transfer its own responsibility as regards public instruction, in matters relating to lower education, to local Governments, and in higher education to such wholly irresponsible bodies as the Presidency Universities — in any country a dangerous, in India positively a perilous, experiment. Such being the case, however, it seems to me time that some one should make known that the Government educational system of the British Government in India is not acceptable to all classes of Her Majesty's Indian subjects, and that the sooner the matter is looked to, the better it will be in the future for England, as well as for India. This, however, is not a general or hap-hazard statement; it can be verified by conclusive proof. The upper classes in the Punjab have rejected the Government system, as is evidenced by their infantile efforts to found a University of their own, independent of it. And that the Musalmáns throughout India will have none of it, was proved to the satisfaction of Lord Mayo by the returns laid before him in 1869, which shewed how miserably small a proportion of Musalmáns were brought under the influence of the Government system. To his Excellency, with his long Irish experience, these results should not have proved startling or even surprising, for to quote from the letter of an English nobleman to me within the past few days, "by the adoption of such a system here you would exclude all good Catholics from Irish posts, as, to be consistent, you would require them to go through Trinity College, or one of the godless colleges, and insist on their passing examinations in Darwin, Huxley, Hegel, and other infidel books." Within the last few months a resolution has issued from the Government of India giving more prominence to the languages of the Musalmáns in the University system; but such legislation is mere trifling with a question of great national importance.*

Being personally concerned, I would prefer to say nothing of the measures proposed by me for the reformed education of the Musalmáns of India; but as you have been good enough to allude to them approvingly, it is due to you that I should briefly explain their principles which, after being accepted by Lords Canning and Halifax, have been set aside in India as unsound. The measures of reform I proposed were so simple that two or three lines will suffice to explain them; and they had this advantage, that they were not only in accordance with the despatches of 1854 and 1859, but in accordance also with the policy of our great European rival in the East—Russia. They were that

* *Vide* Advertisement.

there should be an Oriental Faculty as well as an English Faculty of Arts in the Calcutta University, that all Oriental colleges should be affiliated to it; that in this faculty education, instead of being given in the language of the foreigner, should be given in the languages of the people of the country, their classics taking the place of Latin and Greek, and English, or a sufficient knowledge of it to fit candidates for all Government employments, though a compulsory study, being treated simply as a language; and that all natives, whether Hindoos or Musalmáns, should be free to graduate in the *literis humanioribus* of the East or the West, as they pleased.

Certain persons in the East believed, or affected to believe, that my views were antiquated, that my object was to revive the days of Orientalism, and that the policy I advocated was retrograde. Even here, since my letters to you have been published, it has been asserted by a leading journal (*vide Standard*, 21st inst.) that I have allowed myself to be somewhat carried away by sympathy for "my Mohammadan *protégés*." Ignorant delusion! My sympathies in this matter are neither with Jew nor Gentile, Hindú, Musalmán, nor Christian. They are with peace and good government; and my object is the maintenance of British rule in India on that sure and firm basis which alone will enable the Government to carry out the great work of civilization which Providence in his wisdom has intrusted to the Sovereign of the British Empire and this Nation—the good will and the happiness of a contented people. I repeat that no purely English education that we can give the Musalmáns in India will make them of any use to us, for it will give them *no* influence whatever with their co-religionists.

I contested my position not with the Government of India, but with the Local Government of Bengal, and in no spirit of dogmatism. My opposition consisted in my refusing to carry out a system which was contrary to the existing orders of the Secretary of State, and as injurious to British interests as it was distasteful to the Musalmáns of India, until such time as the whole question of the education of the Musalmáns had been carefully considered by the Government of India and the Secretary of State in Council. I went no further, and I went thus far, because I conceived that a very grave responsibility rested upon all parties adopting a policy of education for twenty or thirty millions of Musalmáns. The question, in my humble judgment, is not one of detail, or involving the practical application of a system approved by the highest authority. It is not one in the philosophy of education which the professors even of a European University could be safely trusted to deal with. It is a question involving political as well as social considerations of singular and serious importance, which the very highest authority alone is competent to decide. A Local Indian Government is plainly not the authority to decide questions of this nature. The Viceroy and Governor-General himself should not finally dispose of a question of this magnitude; and Her Majesty's Secretary of State would act wisely certainly in consulting the ablest men in England before issuing orders on such a subject. M. Guizot did not introduce his Law into the French Chambers without having first sent the lamented Victor Cousin to Prussia, to examine and report on their system of education, and, with all his caution, the results of his measures in France have not justified his expectations. Lord Mayo, I am told, has within the past few months had this question as regards the Mohammadan College of Calcutta before him, and has passed some orders thereon; but it is not too late for the Secretary of State to review, not simply these orders, but the whole question.

And let me add one word in conclusion. It is a common belief that principles are the same all over the world, and that all we have to do in India is to apply those principles of government which have been successful in Europe, or more generally in England. I admit the former, and deny the latter. If principles remain unaltered, it is to their more intelligent application and the adaptation of measures based on them to circumstances which will alone insure success. Many people, and people of great European experience, have grand ideas of the 200,000,000 of Her Majesty's Indian subjects being welded into a great English speaking and English thinking nation, which, sinking distinctions of race and creed, shall take its place in the great family of nationalities of the world. But these philanthropists forget that the Indian Empire is as large as the whole of Europe without Russia, and contains very many nationalities. They forget that circumstances as found in European countries, taking India as a whole, are reversed in Hindostan. They forget that if *l'union fait la force* in European nationalities, in India *l'union fait la faiblesse*, from the British rule stand-point. They forget that the Hindú races extend no further than the limits of Hindostan (*Hindú-isthán*, or place of Hindús), and that while the Hindú is amenable to public opinion as it exists within our own boundaries, the Musalmán races extend over Persia, Arabia, Egypt, European and Asiatic Turkey, Affghanistan, Central Asia, and now part of China. The Musalmán is amenable to the public opinion of his co-religionists over these widely extended regions, and his education must be such as will enable him at least to hold his own and prevent him being taunted as a Hindu, a Christian, or an infidel. They talk about educating the people of India to govern themselves, and they forget that the very measures they propose are those which must insure our being driven out of the country long before that happy period could possibly arrive. Sir Bartle Frere has wisely and well dilated on the difficulties we encounter from the absence of public opinion in India; and if some efforts were made to obtain it, no doubt better government would follow.

Yours faithfully,

W. NASSAU LEES.

Beachlands, Ryde, Isle of Wight, Oct. 30.

Of the Influence exercised on the Education, both University and Popular of England, by the late Prince Consort.

We have before alluded to the secession of the men of the North from the Universities of England in the early part of the seventeenth century, and the subsequent foundation of the University of Edinburgh; and it is not surprising that it was a student of that Institution, Lord John Russell, supported by public opinion, who carried the measure in Parliament to which England is indebted for the new constitutions her two Great Educational Institutions received in 1852. How these constitutions will meet the requirements of the present age, or how those persons entrusted with the responsibility of governing the Universities will adapt them to the altering circumstances of a progressive civilization, it is yet too soon to predict. But, endowed with that spirit of vitality which in all well-regulated institutions of national growth is certain to be inherent, we may hope that the result will not disappoint the expectations of the country, or of those who took a prominent part in initiating and bringing these reforms about.

If to Lord John Russell, however, and to his supporters, is due the merit of having enabled the Crown to exercise its previously doubtful prerogative of instituting enquiries into the management of the affairs of Corporations so influential, so wealthy, and so powerfully protected by the Charters and Letters Patent of ancient Kings and Queens, as the Universities of Oxford and Cambridge, there is another personage to whom is due the more exalted merit of having, long prior to the action of Parliament, appreciated the true principle of elevating the higher education of the Nation; and there is another quarter in which we must seek the origin of those influences which prepared the public mind for the acceptance of changes in the character of venerated institutions —a quarter, too, where, considering the peculiar circumstances of the case, few Englishmen would have expected to find it. We allude to the late illustrious and lamented PRINCE CONSORT.

From the most distant times of which we have any distinct record, whether we ascend to the esoteric teaching of the Pythagoreans, or go back still further to those mysteries of the Egyptians or Indian Brahmins, in which some suppose them to have had their origin; or whether, retracing our steps, we approach gradually through the dark ages down to the borders of the age in which we live, it has been the ruling idea that knowledge is the inheritance of a special class,—the property of the favoured few. Even at the present day, although probably not many would accept the position as we offer it, the number of those who have maintained, and who still maintain, that the education and enlightenment of the upper classes is the *summum bonum*, and that it is to this aim the efforts of a Government ought to be mainly directed, is by no means inconsiderable. "A little leaven leaveneth the whole lump," and so it has been, and is still, supposed by many, that education, if established on high, will percolate downward, permeating the ranks of all classes of the people. But the whole history of civilization demonstrates the falsity of this proposition, the converse of which we have long believed to be true. And although we do not assert that Prince Albert was the first to discover this disputed yet simple truth, or to propound it as a theory; nor that he was even the first person to give prominence to this idea; we do assert that he stood foremost amongst the profound thinkers and distinguished statesmen of his age, in having been the first person in Great Britain to give a *practical* application to the grand principle which this theory involves. The teaching of books, of Schools, of Colleges, and of Universities, may do much for the advancement of learning and science, but these are not the best means of *ennobling* the national mind,—of elevating the tone of a Nation's whole social system,—or of rescuing the great body of the subjects of a State from the practice of demoralizing vices and low and unworthy pursuits and pastimes, which blunt the sensibilities, and degrade man to the level of the brute. Indeed, taking a comprehensive view of the subject, we may almost say that to such ends they are not a means at all. Softer and more gentle influences, influences which, while appealing to those higher qualities of which the human mind, however debased, can never be *totally* devoid, are better adapted for the purpose than the severe teaching of the school-room, the lecture-room, or the cloister, provided always that they are judiciously applied, and practical in their tendencies, or, to speak more intelligibly that, while elevating the mind, they conduce to the greater material prosperity and the greater social happiness of the people.

Now it is a peculiarity of all great educational and social reforms originating with, and encouraged by, Prince Albert, that they were pre-eminently calculated to effect some *solid*—some *real* good. His first consideration, his highest aim, was that the objects he sought to promote should have some useful and practical result. One of the gravest faults of character attributed to the Germans by the English is, that in their undertakings they are not, generally, practical; and it seems passing strange that, in a country like England, a German, and above all, a German Prince, should merit the high honour of having done more towards that immense improvement in agriculture which has taken place of late years, than any other person in it. Nor did he accomplish this end merely by encouraging others, or by lecturing and speaking about the subjects in which he was interested, as most persons in his exalted position would have been content to do. He was amongst the very first not only to appreciate the advantages of deep drainage, the application of steam power, and the resources of chemistry to practical agriculture, but, as a practical agriculturist, himself to demonstrate them. The *practical* was evidently his cherished aim, and in the outlines of the comprehensive plan which he sketched for the accomplishment of the great work he set himself to do, this seems ever to have been kept prominently before his view. That he had such a plan, we are left very little room to doubt. His earnest endeavours to improve the *culture* of the great body of the people, by inspiring within them a taste for the refinements of Music and the Fine Arts ; the deep interest evinced by him in National Education, especially in pointing out the great importance of the cultivation, *by all classes*, of such branches of knowledge, as, by expounding the laws, and unfolding the beautiful truths of Nature, enlarge the mind ; his untiring and unceasing exertions to effect, with the development of intellectual power, the formation, on the most approved model, of the *character* of the labouring classes, are, one and all, so many convincing proofs that his numerous undertakings were not the result of conclusions accidentally or hastily arrived at, but each distinct and separate portions of a happily conceived and well-designed plan for elevating and *ennobling* the Nation. Having early appreciated the fact that, however enlightened and highly cultivated the upper ten thousand may be, no people, as a Nation, can ever become truly great, unless the masses are imbued with a kindred spirit, it required but a small effort of his genius to arrive at the conclusion, that to whatever level in intellectual culture he could raise the middle and lower strata of the population, the higher classes, to hold their own, must *of necessity* be compelled to raise themselves above it. "Let us hope," said he in his speech on laying the foundation stone of the National Gallery of Edinburgh, "that the impulse given to the culture of the Fine Arts in this country, and the daily increasing attention bestowed upon it by the people at large, will not only tend to refine and elevate the national tastes, but will also lead to the production of works, which, if left behind us as memorials of our age, will give to after-generations an adequate idea of our advanced state of civilization."

But we would give a false impression of the distinguished services of the late Prince Consort to the cause of Education, if what we have said should induce any of our readers to suppose that he was unmindful of the claims of higher education on the State, or disposed to leave its amelioration to follow the course of events. As Chancellor of the University of Cambridge, it was undoubtedly, in a great measure, due to his influence, that that Institution evinced a greater readiness than Oxford to correct the abuses which had grown up with the University system of England. Himself, as highly gifted a scholar as he was a refined and an accomplished man, throughout his life, and almost to the last hour of it, he lost no opportunity of indicating the necessity, in an educational system, of attaching due importance to each and every department of knowledge necessary to "perfect the man." On the occasion of laying the first stone of the Birmingham and Midland Institute he said:—"The study of the laws by which the Almighty governs the universe is therefore our bounden duty. *Of these laws our great Academies and seats of education have, rather arbitrarily, selected only two spheres or groups (as I may call them) as essential parts of our national education: the laws which regulate quantities and proportions, which form the subject of Mathematics, and the laws regulating the expression of our thoughts, through the medium of language, that is to say, grammar, which finds its purest expression in the classical language.* These laws are most important branches of knowledge; their study trains and elevates the mind, but they are not the only ones, there are others which we cannot disregard, which we cannot do without."

These, he added, are Logic and Metaphysics, Physiology and Psychology, Politics, Jurisprudence, and Political Economy, and the Physical Sciences. And again, on assuming the Presidentship of the British Association for the Advancement of Science, after dwelling on the difficulties the Association had to contend with in a country similarly circumstanced to England, he said:—"Is it, then, to be wondered at that the interests of Science, abstruse as Science appears, and not immediately shewing a return in pounds, shillings, and pence, should be postponed, at least to others which promise immediate tangible results? Is it to be wondered at that even our public men require an effort to wean themselves from other subjects, in order to give their attention to Science and men of Science, *when it is remembered that Science, with the exception of Mathematics, was, until of late, almost systematically excluded from our School and University education;* that the traditions of early life are those which make and leave the strongest impression on the human mind; and that the subjects with which we become acquainted, and to which our energies are devoted in youth, are those for which we retain the liveliest interest in after years; and that for these reasons the effort required must be both a mental and a moral one?"

We could cull from the admirable discourses of this illustrious Prince many extracts illustrating, from our present stand-point, the high and enlightened principles by which his educational policy was guided, and in proof of the firm and undeviating integrity with which, speaking more generally, he followed that line of conduct which, from the first, he prepared himself to pursue ; but it would be impossible to compress into two short columns a tenth part of them. With a rare combination of ability and energy, patience and perseverance, tact and good sense, he laboured assiduously to accomplish the one great object of his public career, devotion to the highest interests of that Nation whose Sovereign Lady had chosen him to be her Consort Prince; and with such high-minded disinterestedness, and such singular integrity, did he discharge his responsible duties to both, that, sinking his own individuality in that of his Queen, he preferred to receive honor rather as the reflex of the lustre which his own good works had shed around her Throne, than as the just due of one who had been mainly instrumental in diffusing that light from which it emanated. England does not know, England cannot know, the deep debt of gratitude it owes to this virtuous Prince, because the people of England can yet hardly appreciate the great value of the services which he rendered to the Nation. There is, besides, another reason for this ignorance. With all his intellectual superiority, with all the prestige of his exalted rank and position, much good that he effected, and much more that he proposed to effect, was veiled from the public view, by that innate modesty which is peculiarly the type of true nobility, and which was one of the distinguishing features of his character. In the willing attention which the people bestowed on his teaching, and in the patient perseverance with which they laboured in those fields, the fertile resources of which he first pointed out, this good Prince sought his simple but noble reward; and in the abundant harvest, rich in the increase of intellectual power, the moral and social improvement, prosperity, contentment, and happiness of all classes, which has been gathered as the fruit of his labours, he has bequeathed to the nation a legacy more valuable than treasures of gold, and to posterity a testimony of his own worth, more enduring than monuments of brass.

We have extended our remarks beyond our usual limits, but the subject is one so full of mournful interest to Englishmen in all quarters of the globe, that we need make no apology. Had it pleased an all-wise Providence to leave this illustrious Prince amongst us for a longer period, it is impossible to say what further benefits he might not have conferred on Great Britain and her people. As we look back on his whole life, it appears to us to resemble rather a beautiful allegory than that hard reality which we are accustomed to find in the lives of Kings and Princes. Like some pure and limpid stream, gently it seemed to flow onward, extending its rich and fertilizing influences to all things within its reach; gently, having run its course, it passed away, leaving throughout the land wide-spread and beneficial results, but, alas ! in the immediate vicinity of its home, a desolation, the intensity of which ONE alone can comprehend.

Of the futility of attempting, by systems of education, to destroy the nationality of a people.

To make up the Present of all nations there must be a Past. The present, to use the words of the late Prince Consort in his address to the British Association, stands on the shoulders of the past; and if so, upon the shoulders of what past shall we build the present of India? Upon those of the past of Egypt, Babylonia, Assyria, Persia, Greece, Rome; Germany, France, England, or any other modernly civilized nation of the world, or upon the past of India herself ? Surely, if ever there was a country, the past of which is interesting and instructive to the student of history, that country is India. What! exclude from the course of an *Indian* University, the ancient history of that people, who, issuing from our common home, established in a remote land, a civilization, unique in itself, which penetrated as far as Egypt, and beyond it ; forbid its students to recall that period, when, all Europe but a little spot being sunk in barbarism, Alexander the Great, if the records of Megasthenes and Strabo are to be believed, found in India schools of philosophers whose whole life was devoted to the study of the sublimest transcendentalism, the profoundest of all knowledge,—the knowledge of the soul? Are we to hide from our Native students our own belief in the superiority of the race from which they have sprung,—that race, who, having settled amongst savage tribes, reduced rude societies to order, invented letters, and elaborating a wondrously perfect language, laid the very foundations, we may say, of the highest order of philology, and who, having similarly invented numbers, unaided, but by the force of their natural genius, advanced to arithmetic and astronomy, calculated eclipses, and made other accurate astronomical observations? Are we to hold back from those, we fain would elevate, the knowledge that, when all was chaos in Northern Europe, their forefathers had established systems of law, logic, and mental and moral philosophy, which, if at the present day they are considered eccentric, prove them, nevertheless, to be capable of, and at one time to have attained, the very highest mental culture, and *then* to have been possessed of an original, and not a purely imitative genius? Are the names of Manu, Yajnavalkya, Parasara, Viswamitra, Sakya Muni, Kapila, Saunaka, Katyayana, Panini, Kalidasa, Vyasa, Valmiki, and a whole host of others we might mention, to be proscribed, and their great works to be held up to public scorn, or, so to speak, to be burned by the common hangman? Or, to take a nearer retrospect, is that Oriental link to be cut out of the chain which connects the civilization of our own times with that of Ancient Greece? Is it from the pages of Chaucer alone that the students of an Eastern University are to learn that, in *his* day, knowledge in England, as in the rest of Europe, was sought from

——————— olde Esculapius,
And Discorides, and eeke Rufus;
Old Ypocras, Haly, and Galien;
Serapyon, Razis, and Avycen;
Averrois, Damescen, and Constantyn;
Bernard, and Gatisden, and Gilbertyn?

Are our students to be permitted to read in Elphinstone, Mill, Elliot, and others, or in the proceedings of the Asiatic Society, of the foundation of mighty empires, the building of temples, the endowment of colleges, schools, and charitable institutions, the encouragement of learning and men of letters, by the mighty sovereigns who have ruled over this land; to see around them the ruins of canals, roads, fortresses, mosques and mausoleums of the most exquisite architecture, and exhibiting a highly refined taste, and to compare them with that monument of "empty bottles" which it was said, and a very few years back might very justly be said, was all we should leave behind us; to hear such men as Sir William Jones, James Prinsep, Sir W. Macnaghten, Colebrooke, H. H. Wilson, Sir Henry Elliot, and the few scholars British India has produced, attained a European celebrity from their profound knowledge of the Past of India, and yet be expected to believe that that Past is "unmixed evil." In short, having eyes shall they see not, ears shall they hear not, and understanding shall they be dead to those impulses which, be they of creed, of nation, or of race, Nature has implanted in the hearts of all it has endowed with superior intelligence? Impossible! Yet such would really appear to be the visionary idea of the authorities of our chief Indian Educational Institutions. The past of India, her mythology, her religions, her laws, her ancient languages, her literature with its dramas and epics, her logic, her antiquities, have all been carefully excluded from the Calcutta University system;* and, whichever way we view it, what a melancholy parody on that system is it, that before the close of the first decade of the Institution's existence, its Vice-Chancellor has thought it necessary to devote a third of his annual address to a vain endeavour, to wean the students from dwelling on that period of their country's history, which is said to be "unmixed evil." And why is this? Why, we would ask, whether the past of India be good or evil, should the sons of her soil be warned against a practice, which from time immemorial, the natives of all countries have considered one of their dearest privileges? Why, again, should it be deleterious?

* A weak attempt has lately been made to introduce a little Arabic and Sanskrit at what is called the 'little go.'

Or, admitting, for argument sake, the past of India to be *all* evil, and the present *all* good, why should any one having full confidence in the latter, dread a comparison with the former, however highly that comparison might be coloured? We really can see no reason for it; but, on the contrary, every reason why such comparison should be encouraged to the utmost, as the surest means of making the students appreciate those great advantages which they are told they enjoy under British rule.

But a question arises on the threshold of this argument, and of all similar arguments in which the premises are not demonstrable facts or admitted truths,—is the conclusion true? *Is* the Past of India unmixed evil? With the most convincing proofs of the high place in the intellectual history of the world which Ancient India has a right to claim, furnished by early Greek Historians, proofs which European *savans* have verified and increased many fold, and with the institutes of Akbar before us—to which as the Government of India are now defraying the expenses of a new edition, they would probably not be ashamed to own their obligations,—we think, we may spare ourselves the trouble of advancing further evidence to prove the negative of so novel a proposition. The Past of India may be singular according to our notions, and, as with the Past of all nations which recede into very remote antiquity, it may contain much that is repugnant to modern ideas of civilization, but, most certainly, no one with any but a very superficial knowledge of that Past, could be so bold or so rash as to pronounce it unmixed evil. Indeed, could any one succeed in establishing the affirmative of this proposition, we fear that he would prove too much ; for, were it so, it would be impossible to find a circumstance more condemnatory of the present system, than that those brought up under it, preferred to look back with longing eyes to those evil times, than to the bright prospect which, they are so confidently assured, lies before them. Depend upon it, if such is the case, there must be something much more wrong with the *present* than with the *past*, and that the fault lies not with the students, or in the practice by them of any modern tricks which they might have picked up from their European instructors, but that the evil has deeper roots. Depend upon it the Natives of this, or of any other country, will not withdraw their thoughts from the present, to dwell with satisfaction or pride on the past, or to yearn after its *imaginary* blessings, unless they feel the want of some *real* blessing which the present does not supply. The learned Doctor, it appears to us, has overlooked—possibly rather looked over, the true cause of discontent which finds expression in regrets for the past, if it really exists. The educated natives of this country, if we understand their aspirations rightly, have no desire whatever to be astrologers, poets, or chroniclers to mythical Indian Princes of ancient memory, nor do they waste much of their time in comparing the brilliancy of the careers of learned men in ancient and modern India. Taking them at Dr. Maine's high valuation, they are far too astute, and far too sensibly alive to their own interests, to have any such silly notions. What they deplore is, that the *real* Kings, Viceroys, and Princes of British India, have *no* astronomers, poets, or historians, attached to their Courts; and that there are *no* learned men in India. In other words, learning is not encouraged; there is no demand for it, and consequently, it is not produced.

Under Mohammadan rule, there was always a large literary class, spread throughout India. The last vestiges of this class still exist, but they are reduced in circumstances, and are scattered so far and wide, that they may almost be said to have disappeared. The class can obtain no fresh blood, or new life, because, for a man to devote himself to any kind of learning *now*, is to make mendicity his profession—or to starve! The class, therefore, and, with it, all learning, is dying out. This, very probably, is what the educated Natives feel; and it is with this very natural feeling, no doubt, which Sir Donald McLeod, and many who coincide with him in his views regarding the present system of exotic education, have very great sympathy.

Nor do we mean, by anything we have said above, to exalt what is commonly called "Oriental learning" over knowledge of the English language and literature, and Western science. Far from it. We have no desire to keep the Natives of India *down ;* we belong to no particular school; we advocate the views of neither Anglicists nor Orientalists, if any such exist at the present day; we should heartily rejoice to see in India men of learning in *every* branch of knowledge; and it is because we do not find them in *any*, that we think there must be something very rotten in the system Vice-Chancellor Maine has so highly extolled.

Of Lord Macaulay's celebrated Education Minute. Its bright side.

About thirty years ago some sharp passages of arms took place in Calcutta. The battle field was the Committee or Board of Public Instruction. Its members, who were split into two factions commonly known as *Orientalists* and *Anglicists*, were the combatants. The bone of contention between them was £10,000 a year, which was the whole sum then set apart from the revenues of the country for the "revival and promotion of literature and the encouragement of the learned Natives of India, and for the introduction and promotion of a knowledge of the sciences," and over this *bone*, and how it should be disposed of, the combatants, who on both sides numbered amongst their ranks the first men of the day, fought many long and well-contested battles. Previously to 1835 the *Orientalists* had had it all their own way. The money had been expended in printing and publishing valuable Oriental texts, in the stipends of students and the salaries of learned Natives, and in translating into Arabic and Sanskrit, English works of approved merit, on various subjects—historical, mathematical, scientific, &c.

At the close of 1834, however, an event occurred which was destined materially to disturb existing arrangements, and to give a turn to preconceived notions and ideas on the subject of Education. This event was the arrival in India of Thomas Babington Macaulay. He was immediately appointed a Member of this Committee, and his keen eye at once detected very many grave errors in the system of public instruction which had been adopted, and it was under the influence, no doubt, of his views, that one half of the Committee formed themselves into an opposition. Warm discussions were soon raised and much controversy of a bitter and rancorous character followed. Both sides, moreover, exhibited some obstinacy and a good deal of bigotry in the views and opinions they expressed.

The *Orientalists* maintained that "learning," in the Act of Parliament, meant the learning only of the East, and "learned men," those who were profound in this kind of knowledge; and that the Committee of Public Instruction had no authority whatever to devote one rupee of the revenues of the country to any other object. From this position they would not retreat an inch.

The *Anglicists*, on the other hand, were equally uncompromising. They would accept of nothing short of the elimination of all Sanskrit and Arabic from the course of study; the total destruction of all works in these languages, which they asserted to be "waste paper;" the ultimate annihilation of those natives who were learned in them, and the substitution of teachers acquainted with the English language and literature and Western science.

The Committee never met, and the controversy was carried on in voluminous minutes which contain some not over-good logic, and a good deal of strong language; but, as the strength of both parties was very evenly balanced, their battles ended without any result, and in this state the question came before the Supreme Council of India for final decision. Lord Macaulay, besides being a Member of the Committee of Public Instruction, was also a member of the Government, and he took no part in the discussion in Committee of the immediate point which was referred, purposely that he might enter upon it unhampered by any previously expressed opinions when it came before him in Council. This happened on the 2nd February, 1835, and he then wrote his celebrated Education

Minute,—a minute which will live in the memory of all interested in the education of the people of India, probably as long as the language in which it is written. In this remarkable and very able paper, Macaulay threw himself, heart and soul, into the cause of the *Anglicists.* He declared that the wording of the Act left the Government of India perfectly free to spend the existing grant "for the purpose of promoting learning, in any way that might be thought advisable," and quite as competent "to direct that it should no longer be employed in encouraging Arabic and Sanskrit, as to direct that the reward for killing tigers in Mysore should be diminished."

The real question, he said, was, "what is the most useful way of employing it." It was admitted, he stated, that the Vernacular languages of India "contained neither literary nor scientific information, and were so poor and rude, that until enriched from some other quarter, it would be difficult to translate any valuable work into them;" and it could not be denied that "a single shelf of a good European library was worth the whole native literature of India and Arabia;" while, on the other hand, whoever knows the English language "has access to all the vast intellectual wealth which all the wisest nations of the earth have created and hoarded in the course of ninety generations." The question then, he said, was "simply whether, when it is in our power to teach this language, we shall teach languages in which, by universal confession, there are no books on any subject which deserve to be compared to our own; whether, when we can teach European science, we shall teach systems which, by universal confession, whenever they differ from those of Europe differ for the worse; and whether, when we can patronise sound Philosophy and true History, we shall countenance, at the public expense, medical doctrines which would disgrace an English farrier; Astronomy, which would move laughter in girls at an English boarding school; History, abounding with Kings thirty feet high, and reigns thirty thousand years long; and Geography, made up of seas of treacle and seas of butter." "We are not without experience," he added, "to guide us." Had our ancestors, at the great revival of letters among the Western nations at the close of the fifteenth century, acted as the Committee of Public Instruction has hitherto acted; had they neglected the language of Cicero and Tacitus; had they confined their attention to the old dialects of our own island; "had they printed nothing and taught nothing at the Universities but chronicles in Anglo-Saxon and Norman French, would England have been what she now is? What Greek and Latin were to the contemporaries of More and Ascham," said he, "our tongue is to the people of India."

Another instance, he said, was still before our eyes,—Russia, "which, in the time of our grandfathers was probably behind the Punjab, may, in the time of our grandchildren, be pressing close on France and Britain in the career of improvement." "And how," he asked, "was this change effected? Not by flattering national prejudices, not by feeding the mind of the young Muscovite with the old woman's stories which his rude fathers had believed; not by filling his head with lying legends about St. Nicholas; not by encouraging him to study the great question, whether the world was or was not created on the 13th of September; not by calling him a learned native, when he has mastered all these points of knowledge; but by teaching him those foreign languages in which the greatest mass of information had been laid up, and thus putting all that information within his reach. The languages of Western Europe civilized Russia. I cannot doubt that they will do for the Hindoo what they have done for the Tartar."

He combated the argument that Arabic and Sanskrit should be taught, because they were valued and appreciated by the natives, by shewing that a system of stipends was necessary to accomplish their cultivation, or, in other words, that no native would study these languages unless he was paid for it, and that the only way the Committee could get rid of the twenty-three thousand folio and quarto volumes with which their shelves were laden, was by giving them away, and yet they could not give as fast as they printed. In the three years ending December, 1834, he said, the Committee had expended Rs. 60,000 in printing, of which they had realized by sale only Rs. 1000. As for their languages being necessary for the study of Hindu and Mohammadan law, he denied that the argument had any bearing on the question at all, for Parliament had commanded a digest of the laws of India to be prepared, and "as soon as the code was promulgated, the *Shasters* and the *Hidayah* would be useless to a Moonsiff or Sudder Ameen." But the argument which appeared to him most untenable was, that Sanskrit and Arabic should be taught, because "they are the languages in which the sacred books of a hundred millions of people are written." It is confessed, he added, "that a language is barren of useful knowledge. We are to teach it because it is fruitful of monstrous superstitions. We are to teach false history, false astronomy, false medicine, because we find them in company with a false religion. We abstain, and I trust we shall always abstain, from giving any public encouragement to those who are engaged in converting natives to Christianity. And while we act thus, can we reasonably and decently bribe men out of the revenues of the State to waste their youth in learning how they are to purify themselves after touching an ass, or what text of Vedas they are to repeat to expiate the crime of killing a goat?"

"To sum up," continued Macaulay, "I think it

clear that we are not fettered by the Act of Parliament of 1813; that we are not fettered by any pledge expressed or implied; that we are free to employ our funds as we choose; that we ought to employ them in teaching what is best worth knowing; that English is better worth knowing than Sanskrit or Arabic; that the natives are desirous to be taught English, and are not desirous to be taught Sanskrit or Arabic; that neither as the languages of law, nor as the languages of religion, have the Sanskrit and Arabic any peculiar claim to our encouragement; that it is possible to make natives of this country thoroughly good English scholars; and that to this end our efforts ought to be directed."

There was one point, however, in which he cordially concurred with those to whose general views he was opposed; "that with the limited means at the disposal of the Committee, it was impossible to attempt to educate the body of the people," and finally he declined, unless the system was changed, to serve on the Committee. "I conceive," he said, "that we have at present no right to the respectable name of a Board of Public Instruction. We are a Board for wasting public money, for printing books which are of less value than the paper on which they are printed was while it was blank; for giving artificial encouragement to absurd history, absurd metaphysics, absurd physics, and absurd theology; for raising up a breed of scholars who find their scholarship an incumbrance and a blemish, who live on the public while they are receiving their education, and whose education is so utterly useless to them, that when they have received it they must either starve or live on the public all the rest of their lives."

Macaulay, by this celebrated minute, carried the Governor-General and the Council of India along with him, and an ordinance was promulgated which changed the entire system. *Orientalism* was doomed; Oriental learning was henceforth to be allowed to die out, and the English language and literature were to take its place. Macaulay had carried his motion, he had obtained permission to place in the hands of the people of India the key of knowledge; he had put forth his strength to emancipate them from the thraldom of ignorance and errors similar to those which had enveloped Europe in darkness, and he had not done so in vain. He had pleaded for the Native of India being placed in a position to raise himself, intellectually, to a level with his conquerors, and to aspire to share with them in the government of his country, and he had gained his cause. It is undoubtedly due to the influence of his opinions that a system of Public Instruction was adopted, without which the introduction of Railways and Electric Telegraphs into India would have been extremely difficult, if not altogether impossible; and it is due to the same cause that natives are now able to enter the Civil Service, to sit on the same

Bench with an English Chief Justice, and that Government can assign to them so large a share of the highest and most confidential appointments. For these benefits the Government, the Country, and its People, must ever remain deeply indebted to Thomas Babington, Lord Macaulay.

Of Lord Macaulay's celebrated Education Minute. Its dark side.

A few days back we reviewed the celebrated education minute of Lord Macaulay, recording our opinion that very great material benefits had accrued to the Government, the Country, and the People from the adoption of the policy he initiated. The view we have taken of the results of that policy is that, we believe, which has long been held by the larger section of the public, who occupy their attention with this important subject. But the time has come, when, those who heartily and sincerely wish well to the people of India, and who desire to see their education based on a foundation somewhat more solid than that suited to a system destined to fit persons to hold Government situations, must carefully enquire into the soundness of the principles upon which the sudden and complete change effected in the Government policy in 1835 was recommended, and must cautiously examine the arguments urged in support of it, and investigate from an educational as well as a material point of view the results which have been obtained.

Hitherto Lord Macaulay's minute has been considered Law. Lord Auckland and the Court of Directors subsequently pointed out some of his misconceptions ; but, of late years, no one has ventured to dispute its canons. Still, it must be borne in mind, that it was written a few months after the great man landed in India ; that, at that time, the subject of Education, which of all subjects is one which ought to be considered calmly and dispassionately, had unfortunately given rise to a violent controversy ; and that, if it cannot be said that Macaulay was the most prominent member of a faction, it cannot be denied that he entered on the discussion with the feelings, and in the spirit, of a partizan. It was referring to this state of things that Lord Auckland remarked in 1839,—when he was compelled by the dissatisfaction exhibited by the Natives at the uncompromising spirit in which the new policy was carried out, to modify the previous orders on the subject,—" Unhappily, I have found violent differences existing upon the subject of Education, and it was for a time (now I trust past, or fast passing away) a watchword for violent dissensions, and in some measure for the display of personal feelings."

There can be little doubt, it occasionally happens, that, in times of great excitement, not only is the judgment of the ablest men blinded, but their powers of discrimination are weakened ; and it appears to us that there are very many portions of this memorable minute of Macaulay's, which the distinguished author would have run his pen through, had he been called upon to revise it, some years later. It is only on some such supposition that it is conceivable how any discussion could have arisen on the meaning of the Act of Parliament of 1813, which, as it formed the grounds of the controversy, is invested with sufficient importance to warrant our examining it carefully. That Act provided that a certain sum should be set apart "for the revival and promotion of literature, and the encouragement of the learned Natives of India, and for the introduction and promotion of a knowledge of the sciences among the inhabitants of the British territories." This passage is punctuated as above in the Act, but were it not so, the wording of it leaves no room whatever to doubt its meaning. It contains two distinct sentences, and each indicates, as clearly as words can indicate, the intentions of Parliament in framing both. The words "revival and promotion," which are used in the first sentence, in the second are changed into "introduction and promotion," and the whole question consequently, hinges on the relative meanings of the words *revival* and *introduction*. If they are synonymous in signification, Macaulay was right; if they are not, he was wrong. There can be no dispute on the point. What, then, are the meanings of these words; and to whom shall we refer the question? Webster is at hand, so we consult him, leaving others to consult Walker or Johnson if they prefer them. *Revival*, then, says Webster, is "the recall, return, or recovery from a state of neglect, oblivion, obscurity, or depression, as the *revival* of letters or learning?" In other words, the reanimation of something that before existed or was known. And *introduction*, "the act of bringing something into notice, practise, or use; as the *introduction* of new modes of dress or of tillage:" something new, it will be observed, something that had not before existed or was not known. The passage has evidently a double sense; if not, why the change of the word "revival?" Reading the text, then, with the calmness and deliberate consideration which at the present time we are able to give to it, it is plain that there were two separate and distinct objects, for the promotion of which the British Parliament desired a portion of the revenues of this country to be set apart,—one, the promotion of *Oriental* learning, and the encouragement of Natives distinguished for their knowledge of it; and the other, the promotion of *European* science, of which the Natives were then ignorant. The former had previously existed, but under the E. I. Company's Rule had begun to languish,—Parliament wished to *revive* it; the other had never existed,—Parliament wished to *introduce* it. The former could only be *revived*, through the medium of the languages which contained it; the latter, the Vernaculars, being admittedly imperfect, could only be *introduced*, through the medium of a foreign and more perfect language, be it a European or an Asiatic one. The only question, then, which should have been discussed, was, is Sanskrit and Arabic, or English, the better medium for communicating to the Natives of India a knowledge of Western science? This solution of the difficulty, if we can speak of a difficulty where there really appears to have been none, would have led to a proportionate distribution of the grant in support of the two objects Parliament wished to promote and encourage, and not only have simplified matters by leaving the *classical* languages of India still in higher education the languages of literature, and making *English* the language of European science; but, while not interfering with any of the good, would probably have prevented many of the evil consequences which followed the change of system. But, so blinded were the controversialists by prejudice, and so stirred up with anger and excitement, that neither side would hear of a compromise, although, in the strictest accordance with the Law. All must be *black*, or all must be *white*.

After disposing of the legal difficulty, and dilating on the immense value of English literature, "the question," said Macaulay, "is, whether, when we have it in our power to teach this language, we shall teach languages in which, by universal confession, there are no books on any subject which deserve to be compared to our own?" But could not the same be asked of Latin and Greek, and of every ancient language under the sun? Macaulay himself admits it and more, when, a few lines above, in the same minute, he states that "it may safely be said that the literature now extant in that language [English] is of far greater value than all the literature, which three hundred years ago was extant in all the languages of the world together;" and a few lines below, that "the literature of England is now more valuable than that of classical antiquity." He did not propose to abolish the study of the *classical* languages of the West, nor declare that *they* were worthless, though admitting their literature to be inferior to our own. He could not have done so without altogether defeating his own object, for, as one of the most brilliant scholars of his day, he was himself a living instance of the great importance of maintaining, in all University systems, *classical* studies. On the contrary, in a passage which we have quoted in a previous article, he asks,—had our ancestors acted as the Committee of Public Instruction acted prior to his time, had they neglected the language of Cicero and Tacitus, and taught nothing but Chronicles in Anglo-Saxon and Norman French, would England have been what she now is? And here be it observed, he speaks of Greek and Latin as languages, and not as *media* for communicating scientific knowledge.

The prime error committed by the *Orientalists* undoubtedly was in attempting, like the schoolmen of the dark ages, to make foreign and dead languages—for Arabic is as much a dead language in India as Sanskrit—the *media* for communicating to the Natives of India scientific, and in this case, completely new knowledge; but the allusion to Tacitus, Cicero, and the Norman and Saxon Chronicles, precludes the supposition that Macaulay in the passage here alluded to meant more than simply literature. Nor, were it otherwise, would the argument hold good, for Copernicus, Galileo, Kepler, Newton, and the other great discoverers in physical science, did not certainly derive *their* inspiration from the study of the Western classics?

English, urged Macaulay, is to the Natives of India what Latin and Greek were to our ancestors. But this is nothing more than a gross blunder—a blunder which, had he known either of the languages, the study of which he condemned, he would not have committed; but which, even with his undoubted knowledge of the structures of English and the Western *classical* languages, he ought to have been ashamed to make. English does *not* stand in the same relation to the people of India as Latin and Greek did to the people of England in the sixteenth or any other century of the Christian era. It is Sanskrit and Arabic which hold that place, and precisely that place, in India, which Macaulay claimed for Latin and Greek in England. Anglo-Saxon and Norman French were the Vernacular languages of England; and, as our ancestors set them aside for Latin and Greek, which were the *classical* languages, not only of England, but of all Europe, so did the Committee of Public Instruction propose to set aside Hindoostani, Bengali, Marhatta, &c., or the Vernacular languages of India, in favour of Arabic and Sanskrit, which are the *classical* languages of the East. We by no means wish to uphold the action of the Orientalists at the period referred to in all respects, for we think bigotry of any kind is hateful; but in this instance they certainly had both reason and right on their side.

Again, as regards the illustration drawn from the educational policy of Russia, it seems to us more unfortunate still; for, firstly, the Russians had no ancient literature; and, secondly, without denying that benefits resulted from the introduction into that country of French and German literature, it is, nevertheless, a fact, that the Russian Government has long since discovered reasons for concluding its policy in this respect to have been a mistaken one, and, for the last fifteen or twenty years, it has been making the most active exertions to repair its error, by reviving the study of the language of the country, and encouraging its cultivation.

Moreover it has done this, not only with the full concurrence of its subjects, but to their great happiness, contentment, and satisfaction, which with all Governments ought certainly to be an important consideration.

Every people prefers its own language to the language of foreigners; it is natural that they should do so, and it is unwise to suppose that the people of India are an exception, or that in this respect they differ from any other people of ancient civilization who have a literature they can call their own. Sanskrit and Arabic, it may be said, are not the languages of India, and it is true that they are not the *living* languages of India; but, for centuries they have been the languages of its schools and colleges, and are the languages which contain the literature of the people,—a literature which, if others despise, they very highly prize. It is no argument at all to say, that, because youths have to be paid for learning these languages, the natives of India do not appreciate them. Such is the custom of the country, and at the present day every wealthy Mohammadan in this city supports two, three, or four students, while they are prosecuting their studies in Arabic.

But there is a very much simpler solution of the paradox. Under British rule there has *lately* been no demand for Oriental scholarship, and it would have been almost as unreasonable to expect the Natives to pay for learning English in the days of

Akbar and Shah Jehan, as to pay for learning Arabic and Sanskrit in the days of Lord William Bentinck and Lord Macaulay. *Il faut vivire* is a necessity which Nature has imposed upon the people of the East, equally with the people of the West, and it is a necessity, in regard to the *poor*, which the *rich* everywhere must recognise. It seems, then, hardly generous or even just to peoples whose Kings and Princes have been deprived of their inheritance and humbled in the dust, and whose rich men have been reduced to a state bordering on poverty, for those who have compassed their overthrow, to turn on them and accuse them of want of appreciation of a thing, because they neglect it to purchase that which, under the new *régime*, alone will give them bread.

But if this is unjust, how far worse than unjust—how bitterly harsh and cruel is that sentiment, which led Macaulay to consider the argument "*that Arabic and Sanscrit should be taught, because they are the languages in which the Sacred Books of a hundred millions of people are written,*" as the most untenable of all the arguments advanced by his opponents. We abstain, said he, from giving public encouragement to those engaged in converting the natives to Christianity, and we are to bribe men out of the revenues of the country, to waste their youth in learning their own Scriptures. On reading this passage, one feels almost tempted to suspect that Macaulay had been so short a time in India when he penned the portion of his minute in which it occurs, that he must have forgotten of what country he was speaking, and what was the main source whence those revenues were derived regarding the proper distribution of which, he expressed such confident opinions. It was our desire to pass over in silence the many contemptuous remarks regarding the institutions of the people of India, and especially their religions, which disfigure this, in other respects, very ably written State paper, because they weaken rather than strengthen the arguments advanced; and we are certain, as before mentioned, that, had Lord Macaulay himself had an opportunity, some years later, of revising his minute, he would have expunged much which, in calmer mood, he could not have approved. But a fallacy lies concealed in this argument, which, as it is still believed in by a very large and influential class both in England and India, we think it well to dispose of. Lord Macaulay has taken great credit for the neutrality of the Government of India of his day in religious matters; but whether, when we refuse to give pecuniary support to men engaged in converting natives to what *we* believe to be the true religion, we are to spend the revenues of the country on men engaged in learning and in teaching idolatry and superstition, was not then, nor is it now, the question with which we have to deal; or, were it so, there are certainly other ways of looking at it.

The questions, from this point of view, for instance, which first occur to us would be;—are we to take from the people of this country £47,000,000 of annual revenue for the purposes of the Government of the country, and allow not *one rupee* of those millions, the greater portion of which has been raised by the sweat of their brows, for the maintenance of their religious institutions? Are we to spend annually out of these revenues £150,000 on bishops, priests, deacons, and ecclesiastical establishments, maintained solely for the spiritual welfare of a few thousand Englishmen, and leave the 150,000,000 of our Hindú and Mohammadan subjects, to provide for the care of their own souls out of the pittance our Revenue collectors may leave them for their private purposes, on the plea that their religions are monstrous superstitions? Are we to lay out annually, and to take immense credit for so doing, £660,000 of those revenues mainly in teaching them our own language and literature, for which the great body of the natives of India do not, and never can, care one straw,—a large portion of which, moreover, is paid to Societies and men with whom conversion to Christianity is confessedly a primary object, and Education, if an object at all, but a means to what they consider a far higher end,—and yet grudge a few hundred pounds a month for teaching the languages which contain the Religion and Laws of our native subjects? Are we to do all these things, and others we might mention, and still prate of the tolerance of British Rule, and glory over the strictness and impartiality with which we observe our traditional policy of perfect Neutrality in matters relating to Religion? Far better would it have been to leave Christianity and Monstrous Superstition out of the account, for if this is Neutrality, it is Neutrality with a vengeance indeed.

As before mentioned, we are no bigots; but our abhorrence of bigotry is not one-sided, nor is it confined to any particular colour or creed. It is universal. We prefer to look at National questions, whether they be political, religious, or educational, from the broad platform of the Statesman, rather than from the narrow grating of the cloister; and in discussing them, to shew as much consideration for the feelings and wishes of the Hindú and Mohammadan, as for those of the Christian and the Jew. We yield to none in our high appreciation of the English language and literature; we admit to the full the benefits that have accrued to the country and the people from the impulse given to the study of that language since 1835; and we look forward, not only with some national pride, but with sincere and unfeigned satisfaction, to the further benefits which will flow from continuing to encourage its cultivation. We, nevertheless, maintain that it is not, and never has been, the policy of the British Parliament, directly or indirectly, to deprive the natives of India of the opportunities, and, consequently, of the means of acquiring a knowledge of the languages in which their Scriptures are written; that, consequently, Macaulay misread the Act of Parliament he essayed to interpret, and thereby misled the Indian Government of the day; that, in viewing the question solely as one of the comparative values of the literatures extant in the English language and the classical languages of the East, and completely ignoring all consideration of the value of the latter as a means of mental culture and discipline, he committed an egregious blunder in the philosophy of education,—a blunder which sooner or later the Government of India must be at great pains and labour and some expense to repair; and that in rudely and violently disregarding the national and religious feelings of our native subjects, he committed an equally grave political error, by causing the Government, of which he was a member, to violate the soundest principle of its Constitution,—that of basing the stability of British rule in India, on the happiness and contentment of the people.

Of the impossibility of giving a National basis to a system of Public Instruction, in which National Institutions and National Feelings are ignored.

In our review of the Education Minute of Lord Macaulay, we pointed out that the sudden change of system introduced into India in 1835, was not in accordance with the provisions of the Act of Parliament, and was consequently, in our opinion, illegal; that the error of the *Anglicists* and *Orientalists* lay, in both parties rushing into extremes; and that, according to the rule in such cases, the correct course, and in this instance the legal course, lay between these extremes. Some of the mischief premeditated, however, was arrested, by Lord Auckland, who desired to shew more consideration for the feelings and wishes of the Natives, and, with the view of effecting the transition from *Orientalism* to *Anglicism* more gently, to maintain existing means for affording the Natives opportunities of learning their own classical languages and literature. Still much was done that was thought, and is still thought, by the Natives, to have been harsh and unjust. In some instances bequests made by Natives for the promotion of Oriental learning, were appropriated for English education, which was very naturally considered little short of spoliation. This certainly was unwise, for it was a wrong,—and it is a wrong which, notwithstanding the enormously increased Parliamentary grant, still continues. More unwisely still, an exclusiveness was set up which was fatal to that harmony and union which alone can insure strength, and which is so essential to the success of every great national movement—an exclusiveness which, though always a charge preferred against the Orientalists, was, in truth, one which, with a greater show of justice, could be urged against the *Anglicists.* The high classes of Hindús, from caste prejudices may have objected to the lower classes sitting on the same benches with them, and Mohammadans may have had religious scruples on the subject of English education ; but neither, we believe, would have objected to receive as much English as was good for them, provided it had been combined with instruction in their own classics, and that greater consideration had been shewn for their religious feelings, as well as more judgment in the application of a system which, as being opposed to their preconceived notions on the subject, was distasteful to them.

Deep-rooted prejudices cannot be overcome in an hour, a day, or a year. Time, patience, and perseverance are necessary to the attainment of the end, provided its accomplishment is intended to be effected without violence. It has been said, and truly said, that nothing would be so painful to a blind man, as to be suddenly restored to sight in the bright light of noon-day. And the illustration is applicable to almost all mental, equally with all bodily, sensations. Macaulay asserted the position to be that of a people of highly intellectual attainments, called upon to superintend the education of a people comparatively ignorant, and he objected that the learners should prescribe the course the teachers ought to take. He looked upon the languages and literatures of the East as a diseased limb, and he proposed to cut it off. But he not only under-rated the intellectual attainments of the learned Natives, and undervalued their languages and literature, but he forgot that with a skilful surgeon, cure is a primary consideration, and amputation a last resource,—a remedy seldom or never, moreover, applied without the consent of the patient.

Writers in this journal, and speakers elsewhere, on the subject we have undertaken to review, have spoken of the question of to-day as a revival of the controversy between *Orientalists* and *Anglicists;* but they are altogether mistaken. That the arguments of those who view the subject from Sir Donald McLeod's stand-point, appear to be directed against the principles of the *Anglicists* may be true; but that such should be the case is unavoidable, because this faction, having gained the upper hand in the struggle of thirty years back, their principles were, in great part, adopted as the basis of the new system then brought into operation. But neither *Orientalism* nor *Anglicism* have anything whatever to do with the question of to-day. That question is not which of the controversialists of 1835 was in the right ; but whether or not the principles of the system of higher education then laid down, and which, speaking generally, have been acted upon ever since, are sound; and the first and most essential qualification in any one who desires to discuss this question on its merits and without prejudice, is the admission that both *Orientalists* and *Anglicists* were, if not wholly, in great part in the wrong.

The movement which has lately taken place in the Punjab, and which has obtained the support of the Lieutenant-Governor of that Province, and of His Excellency the Governor-General, has nothing to do with party feeling of any kind. It is simply a spontaneous effort on the part of the native nobility and gentry of the Punjab to revive the cultivation of the classical languages of India—or, in other words, to carry into effect an important part of the provisions of the Act of Parliament of 1813, which we have shewn pretty clearly in a previous article the Indian Government of the day either misunderstood or misinterpreted. How the promoters of this movement will carry their views into effect remains to be seen; but the movement has not originated with Government,—it comes from within, and is therefore entitled to more respect than ordinary movements of the kind, which originate usually in pressure from without, and embody little more than official inspiration. It is supported by a large, respectable, and influential body of our Native subjects, and as clearly indicating their disapproval of the existing Government system of education, is invested with an importance, and has a significance which renders it desirable that it should receive attention.

We entertain the profoundest admiration for Lord Macaulay's brilliant talents ; but without any wish to detract from his great merits, we may say that by this time it is, or ought to be known, that at no period of his career had he sufficient Indian experience to lay down a project for the reform of any department of the administration of Indian affairs, which could be adopted in full detail, with any reasonable prospect of success. Had his Penal Code been put in force at the time he drafted it, we have no hesitation in saying that, instead of being beneficial, it would have been mischievous in its effects ; and had it, at any time, been adopted in the form in which he left it, it would have broken down almost as soon as it was promulgated. The same may be said of his scheme for officering the Civil Service of India ; and that his Educational views, which were put forth a few months after he landed in India, should have been such as could safely be adopted throughout India in their integrity, without modification or adaptation, is hardly to be expected. All honour is due to Lord Macaulay for his powerful advocacy of the claims of our

Indian subjects to be afforded, not only opportunities, but ample means for acquiring a language which would give them access to that knowledge, which has made the people of England a great Nation. But the grammar and structure of the English language are not such as to render it, as a mental discipline, suitable for replacing Latin and Greek or Arabic and Sanskrit ; and, as before pointed out, here was a weakness in the basement of the system, which, it should have been self-evident from the very outset, unfitted it to bear the weight of a solid superstructure. Yet, if it can be said that this was a defect sufficiently important to have raised serious doubts as to the success of the scheme, another error was committed which, looking at the question from a National point of view, was such as to place success beyond the bounds of possibility.

In 1835 the Overland Route had not been established, and India was, in point of time, very much further then than it is now from Europe. It therefore probably did not attract the attention of the Indian Government of the day, that when the discussion of this great question came on in Calcutta, the foundations of a National system of Public Instruction had just been laid down in France ; and it consequently did not occur to them to compare the opinions submitted for their consideration by Macaulay, with those expressed by men in Europe, who, if not his superiors in oratorical power and mastery over language, were certainly so in knowledge of the subject under consideration and in statesmanship. We allude to the distinguished Educationist and Author, M. Victor Cousin and M. Guizot. Let us see how the reformers acted in the East and the West, not under circumstances wholly dissimilar.

Macaulay came to India and found a tree as it appeared to him barren of fruit; he waited not three years, nay, hardly three months,—he stayed not to dig about it, nor to dung it, but said at once, "Cut it down, why cumbereth it the ground?"

What, on the other hand, did M. Guizot do? He sent Victor Cousin, one of the most profound and popular writers of the age, into Prussia, which was then that country of Europe in which education had received the greatest development, to make the most careful investigation into the Prussian system, and to acquaint himself with its results. M. Guizot was satisfied from M. Cousin's report of the soundness of the Prussian system of National Education, but nevertheless he did not, on that account, attempt to transplant it in its integrity into France. He adapted it to the Institutions of his country, and framed a modification of it which he thought would be more in accordance with the feelings and wishes of his countrymen, and which consequently, as a National measure, would afford more reasonable hopes of success. "Nothing," said M. Victor Cousin in his Report to the Minister, "must pass into *Law* which has not the warranty of success. *Laws* are not to be perilous experiments on society; they ought simply to sum up and to generalize the lessons of experience." And again:—"I wish for a *Law*, and at the same time I dread it; for I tremble, lest we should plunge into visionary and impracticable projects again, *without attending to what actually exists.*" And M. Guizot repeated the same sentiments, when, in introducing his measure to the Chamber of Deputies in 1832, he said:—"We conceive that, on the subject of the education of the people, our business is to methodize and improve what exists, rather than to destroy, for the purpose of inventing and renewing upon the faith of dangerous theories."

These great reformers saw at once that, however defective an existing system might be, violently to tear it up by the roots, would outrage the feelings of all who had been brought up under it, and whose co-operation was especially essential to their success. The Clergy were especially to be conciliated. "We *must* have the Clergy," said Victor Cousin; but how did he propose to associate them with him in the business of reform? "We must neither deliver over our Committees," said he, "into the hands of the Clergy, nor exclude them; we must admit them, *because they have a right to be there, and to represent the religion of the people.*"

Had the Indian Government of 1835-36 carried

out their measures of reform in the same spirit, and with the same cautious forethought,—had they shewn the same consideration for the religions of the people, and for those who represented them,—had they recognized what was good in that which existed, and rejected only what was bad, superadding anything else they pleased,—had they been content to introduce their reforms as steadily, but still more gradually, and with a stricter regard to maintain the great principle of *Union*,—they would have carried the whole country along with them, and, it is difficult now to say, what great results would not have been attained. But no; all these considerations, the observance of which, to give the system a National basis, was of the essence of success, were ignored. The learning which our Native subjects not only respected but revered, was condemned as worse than worthless; their books were pronounced to be of less value than the paper on which they were printed whilst it was blank; their *Pundits* and *Moulavies*,—the Clergy of India,—were declared to be ignorant and incompetent; and their religions not only reviled but ridiculed as monstrous superstitions. It is not such means which have ever proved successful in leading a Nation from the paths of error to the paths of truth; because such arguments are, least of all, likely to carry conviction home to the minds of any people imbued with strong prejudices. The opportunity, then, of founding a *National* system of education for India, if it had arrived, was lost ; and no attempt has since been made to improve it. The terms *Oriental* and *English* Colleges still remain, indices of the disunion which was effected thirty years ago—beacons to warn future Governments of India off that fatal rock, upon which the State vessel which carries the best fortunes of the Empire was then wrecked.

Some are impressed with the idea that, because twelve or fifteen hundred students annually enter themselves for the Examinations of the Calcutta University, it is a popular institution ; but this is a mischievous mistake. The Presidency College, though always an English College, and though its foundation was opposed, remained a popular Institution, because it was raised on the foundation of the old Hindú College which the Natives had learned to appreciate and respect ; the Sanskrit College and the Madrassah, notwithstanding that religion and the sciences have been excluded, are still popular, because they were given, at their foundation, a Constitution which was agreeable to the Natives, and because they still retain a portion of their former prestige. But the Presidency College for some reason or other, is fast losing its popularity, the Sanskrit College is being gradually absorbed into this College ; and strong efforts have been repeatedly made to abolish the Hooghly and Calcutta Madrassahs altogether. The Calcutta University is *not* popular, and we doubt if it ever will be popular. It would have collapsed at the outset had not its examinations been made the tests for all the Government School and College scholarships in the Presidency. Were the number of these scholarships largely increased, the number of candidates for entrance would soon be doubled; were its licenses and certificates a *certain* passport to a Government clerkship, more rapidly still would they be quadrupled. As it is, their number will ere long be so large, that no machinery the Government of India can provide will be equal to conducting the University examinations with any species of integrity.

But all this is no indication of popularity; for there can be little doubt that, were Government to appoint Chinese as the test for appointments in their service, instruction in it would be as eagerly sought and as readily paid for, as for what is now called an English education. But would any one, from this fact, be justified in concluding that the study of the Chinese language was popular with the people of India? No!

APPENDIX.

LORD MACAULAY'S MINUTE.

"*2nd February*, 1835.

"As it seems to be the opinion of the gentlemen who compose the Committee of Public Instruction, that the course which they have hitherto pursued was strictly prescribed by the British Parliament in 1813, and as, if that opinion be correct, a legislative Act will be necessary to warrant a change, I have thought it right to refrain from taking any part in the preparation of the adverse statements which are now before us, and to reserve what I had to say on the subject till it should come before me as a member of the Council of India.

"It does not appear to me that the Act of Parliament can, by any art of construction, be made to bear the meaning which has been assigned to it. It contains nothing about the particular languages or sciences which are to be studied. A sum is set apart 'for the revival and promotion of literature and the encouragement of the learned natives of India, and for the introduction and promotion of a knowledge of the sciences among the inhabitants of the British territories.' It is argued, or rather taken for granted, that by literature the Parliament can have only meant Arabic and Sanscrit literature, that they never would have given the honourable appellation of a 'learned native' to a native who was familiar with the poetry of Milton, the metaphysics of Locke, and the physics of Newton; but that they meant to designate by that name only such persons as might have studied in the sacred books of the Hindoos all the usages of cusa-grass, and all the mysteries of absorption into the Deity. This does not appear to be a very satisfactory interpretation. To take a parallel case; suppose that the Pacha of Egypt, a country once superior in knowledge to the nations of Europe, but now sunk far below them, were to appropriate a sum for the purpose of 'reviving and promoting literature, and encouraging learned natives of Egypt,' would anybody infer that he meant the youth of his pachalic to give years to the study of hieroglyphics, to search into all the doctrines disguised under the fable of Osiris, and to ascertain with all possible accuracy the ritual with which cats and onions were anciently adored? Would he be justly charged with inconsistency, if, instead of employing his young subjects in deciphering obelisks, he were to order them to be instructed in the English and French languages, and in all the sciences to which those languages are the chief keys?

"The words on which the supporters of the old system rely do not bear them out, and other words follow which seem to be quite decisive on the other side. This lac of rupees is set apart, not only for 'reviving literature in India,' the phrase on which their whole interpretation is founded, but also for 'the introduction and promotion of a knowledge of the sciences among the inhabitants of the British territories,'—words which are alone sufficient to authorize all the changes for which I contend.

"If the Council agree in my construction, no legislative Act will be necessary. If they differ from me, I will prepare a short Act rescinding that clause of the Charter of 1813, from which the difficulty aries.

"The argument which I have been considering affects

only the form of proceeding. But the admirers of the Oriental system of education have used another argument, which, if we admit it to be valid, is decisive against all change. They conceive that the public faith is pledged to the present system, and that to alter the appropriation of any of the funds which have hitherto been spent in encouraging the study of Arabic and Sanscrit would be downright spoliation. It is not easy to understand by what process of reasoning they can have arrived at this conclusion. The grants which are made from the public purse for the encouragement of literature differed in no respect from the grants which are made from the same purse for other objects of real or supposed utility. We found a sanatarium on a spot which we suppose to be healthy. Do we thereby pledge ourselves to keep a sanatarium there, if the result should not answer our expectation? We commence the erection of a pier. Is it a violation of the public faith to stop the works, if we afterwards see reason to believe that the building will be useless? The rights of property are undoubtedly sacred. But nothing endangers those rights so much as the practice, now unhappily too common, of attributing them to things to which they do not belong. Those who would impart to abuses the sanctity of property are in truth imparting to the institution of property the unpopularity and fragility of abuses. If the Government has given to any person a formal assurance; nay, if the Government has excited in any person's mind a reasonable expectation that he shall receive a certain income as a teacher or a learner of Sanscrit or Arabic, I would respect that person's pecuniary interests—I would rather err on the side of liberality to individuals than suffer the public faith to be called in question. But to talk of a Government pledging itself to teach certain languages and certain sciences, though those languages may become useless, though those sciences may be exploded, seems to me quite unmeaning. There is not a single word in any public instructions from which it can be inferred that the Indian Government ever intended to give any pledge on this subject, or ever considered the destination of these funds as unalterably fixed. But, had it been otherwise, I should have denied the competence of our predecessors to bind us by any pledge on such a subject. Suppose that a Government had in the last century enacted in the most solemn manner that all its subjects should, to the end of time, be inoculated for the small-pox: would that Government be bound to persist in the practice after Jenner's discovery? These promises, of which nobody claims the performance, and from which nobody can grant a release; these vested rights, which vest in nobody; this property without proprietors; this robbery, which makes nobody poorer, may be comprehended by persons of higher faculties than mine—I consider this merely as a set form of words, regularly used both in England and India, in defence of every abuse for which no other plea can be set up.

"I hold this lac of rupees to be quite at the disposal of the Governor-General in Council, for the purpose of promoting learning in India, in any way which may be thought most advisable. I hold his Lordship to be quite as free to direct that it shall no longer be employed in encouraging Arabic and Sanscrit, as he is to direct that the reward for killing tigers in Mysore shall be diminished, or that no more public money shall be expended on the chanting at the cathedral.

"We now come to the gist of the matter. We have a fund to be employed as Government shall direct for the intellectual improvement of the people of this country.

The simple question is, what is the most useful way of employing it?

"All parties seem to be agreed on one point, that the dialects commonly spoken among the natives of this part of India contain neither literary or scientific information, and are, moreover so poor and rude that, until they are enriched from some other quarter, it will not be easy to translate any valuable work into them. It seems to be admitted on all sides that the intellectual improvement of those classes of the people who have the means of pursuing higher studies can at present be effected only by means of some language not vernacular amongst them.

"What, then, shall that language be? One half of the Committee maintain that it should be the English. The other half strongly recommend the Arabic and Sanscrit. The whole question seems to me to be, which language is the best worth knowing?

"I have no knowledge of either Sanscrit or Arabic.—But I have done what I could to form a correct estimate of their value. I have read translations of the most celebrated Arabic and Sanscrit works. I have conversed both here and at home with men distinguished by their proficiency in the Eastern tongues. I am quite ready to take the Oriental learning at the valuation of the Orientalists themselves. I have never found one among them who could deny that a single shelf of a good European library was worth the whole native literature of India and Arabia. The intrinsic superiority of the Western literature is, indeed, fully admitted by those members of the Committee who support the Oriental plan of education.

"It will hardly be disputed, I suppose, that the department of literature in which the Eastern writers stand highest is poetry. And I certainly never met with any Orientalist who ventured to maintain that the Arabic and

Sanscrit poetry could be compared to that of the great European nations. But, when we pass from works of imagination to works in which facts are recorded and general principles investigated, the superiority of the Europeans becomes absolutely immeasurable. It is, I believe, no exaggeration to say, that all the historical information which has been collected from all the books written in the Sanscrit language is less valuable that what may be found in the most paltry abridgments used at preparatory schools in England. In every branch of physical or moral philosophy the relative position of the two nations is nearly the same.

"How, then, stands the case? We have to educate a people who cannot at present be educated by means of their mother-tongue. We must teach them some foreign language. The claims of our own language it is hardly necessarily to recapitulate. It stands pre-eminent even among the languages of the West. It abounds with works of imagination not inferior to the noblest which Greece has bequeathed to us; with models of every species of eloquence; with historical compositions, which, considered merely as narratives, have seldom been surpassed, and which, considered as vehicles of ethical and political instruction, have never been equalled; with just and lively representations of human life and human nature; with the most profound speculations on metaphysics, morals, government, jurisprudence, and trade; with full and correct information respecting every experimental science which tends to preserve the health, to increase the comfort, or to expand the intellect of man. Whoever knows that language, has ready access to all the vast intellectual wealth, which all the wisest nations of the earth have created and hoarded in the course of ninety generations. It may safely be said that the literature now extant in that language is of far greater value than all the literature which three hundred years ago was extant in all the languages of the world together. Nor is this all. In India, English is the language spoken by the ruling class. It is spoken by the higher class of natives at the seats of Government. It is likely to become the language of commerce throughout the seas of the East. It is the language of two great European communities which are rising, the one in the south of Africa, the other in Australasia; communities which are every year becoming more important, and more closely connected with our Indian empire. Whether we look at the intrinsic value of our literature, or at the particular situation of this country, we shall see the strongest reason to think that, of all foreign tongues, the English tongue is that which would be the most useful to our native subjects.

"The question now before us is simply whether, when it is in our power to teach this language, we shall teach languages in which, by universal confession, there are no books on any subject which deserve to be compared to our own; whether, when we can teach European science, we shall teach systems which, by universal confession, whenever they differ from those of Europe, differ for the worse; and whether, when we can patronise sound Philosophy and true History, we shall countenance, at the public expense, medical doctrines which would disgrace an English Farrier—Astronomy, which would move laughter in girls at an English boarding school—History, abounding with kings thirty feet high, and reigns thirty thousand years long—and Geography, made up of seas of treacle and seas of butter.

"We are not without experience to guide us. History furnishes several analogous cases, and they all teach the same lesson. There are in modern times, to go no further, two memorable instances of a great impulse given to the mind of a whole society—of prejudices overthrown—of knowledge diffused—of taste purified—of arts and sciences planted in countries which had recently been ignorant and barbarous.

"The first instance to which I refer is the great revival of letters among the Western nations at the close of the fifteenth and the beginning of the sixteenth century. At that time almost everything that was worth reading was contained in the writings of the ancient Greeks and Romans. Had our ancestors acted as the Committee of Public Instruction has hitherto acted; had they neglected the language of Cicero and Tacitus; had they confined their attention to the old dialects of our own island; had they printed nothing and taught nothing at the universities but Chronicles in Anglo-Saxon and Romances in Norman-French, would England have been what she now is? What the Greek and Latin were to the contemporaries of More and Ascham, our tongue is to the people of India. The literature of England is now more valuable than that of classical antiquity. I doubt whether the Sanscrit literature be as valuable as that of our Saxon and Norman progenitors. In some departments—in History, for example—I am certain that it is much less so.

"Another instance may be said to be still before our eyes. Within the last hundred and twenty years, a nation which had previously been in a state as barbarous as that in which our ancestors were before the Crusades, has gradually emerged from the ignorance in which it was sunk, and has taken its place among civilised communities —I speak of Russia. There is now in that country a large educated class, abounding with persons fit to serve the state in the highest functions, and in nowise inferior to the most accomplished men who adorn the best circles of

Paris and London. There is reason to hope that this vast empire, which in the time of our grandfathers was probably behind the Punjab, may, in the time of our grandchildren, be pressing close on France and Britain in the career of improvement. And how was this change effected? Not by flattering national prejudices; not by feeding the mind of the young Muscovite with the old woman's stories which his rude fathers had believed: not by filling his head with lying legends about St. Nicholas: not by encouraging him to study the great question, whether the world was or was not created on the 13th of September: not by calling him 'a learned native,' when he has mastered all these points of knowledge: but by teaching him those foreign languages in which the greatest mass of information had been laid up, and thus putting all that information within his reach. The languages of Western Europe civilized Russia. I cannot doubt that they will do for the Hindoo what they have done for the Tartar.

"And what are the arguments against that course which seems to be alike recommended by theory and by experience? It is said that we ought to secure the co-operation of the native public, and that we can do this only by teaching Sanscrit and Arabic.

"I can by no means admit that, when a nation of high intellectual attainments undertakes to superintend the education of a nation comparatively ignorant, the learners are absolutely to prescribe the course which is to be taken by the teachers. It is not necessary, however, to say anything on this subject. For it is proved by unanswerable evidence that we are not at present securing the co-operation of the natives. It would be bad enough to consult their intellectual taste at the expense of their intellectual health. But we are consulting neither—we are withholding from them the learning for which they are craving; we are forcing on them the mock-learning which they nauseate.

"This is proved by the fact that we are forced to pay our Arabic and Sanscrit students, while those who learn English are willing to pay us. All the declamations in the world about the love and reverence of the natives for their sacred dialects will never, in the mind of any impartial person, outweigh the undisputed fact, that we cannot find, in all our vast empire, a single student who will let us teach him those dialects unless we will pay him.

"I have now before me the accounts of the Madrassa for one month—the month of December, 1833. The Arabic students appear to have been seventy-seven in number. All receive stipends from the public. The whole amount paid to them is above 500 rupees a month. On the other side of the account stands the following item: Deduct amount realized from the out-students of English for the months of May, June, and July last, 103 rupees.

"I have been told that it is merely from want of local experience that I am surprised at these phenomena, and that it is not the fashion for students in India to study at their own charges. This only confirms me in my opinion. Nothing is more certain than that it never can in any part of the world be necessary to pay men for doing what they think pleasant and profitable. India is no exception to this rule. The people of India do not require to be paid for eating rice when they are hungry, or for wearing woollen cloth in the cold season. To come nearer to the case before us, the children who learn their letters and a little elementary Arithmetic from the village schoolmaster are not paid by him. He is paid for teaching them. Why, then, is it necessary to pay people to learn Sanscrit and Arabic? Evidently because it is universally felt that the Sanscrit and Arabic are languages the knowledge of which does not compensate for the trouble of acquiring them. On all such subjects the state of the market is the decisive test.

"Other evidence is not wanting, if other evidence were required. A petition was presented last year to the Committee by several ex-students of the Sanscrit College. The petitioners stated they had studied in the college ten or twelve years; that they had made themselves acquainted with Hindoo literature and science; that they had received certificates of proficiency: and what is the fruit of all this? 'Notwithstanding such testimonials,' they say, 'we have but little prospect of bettering our condition without the kind assistance of your Honourable Committee, the indifference with which we are generally looked upon by our countrymen leaving no hope of encouragement and assistance from them.' They therefore beg that they may be recommended to the Governor-General for places under the Government, not places of high dignity or emolument, but such as may just enable them to exist. 'We want means,' they say, 'for a decent living, and for our progressive improvement, which, however, we cannot obtain without the assistance of Government, by whom we have been educated and maintained from childhood.' They conclude by representing, very pathetically, that they are sure that it was never the intention of Government, after behaving so liberally to them during their education, to abandon them to destitution and neglect.

"I have been used to see petitions to Government for compensation. All these petitions, even the most unreasonable of them, proceeded on the supposition that some loss had been sustained—that some wrong had been inflicted. These are surely the first petitioners who ever demanded compensation for having been educated gratis—for having been supported by the public during twelve years, and then sent forth into the world well furnished with literature and science. They represent their education as an injury which gives them a claim on the Government for redress, as an injury, for which the stipends paid to them during the infliction were a very inadequate compensation. And I doubt not that they are in the right. They have wasted the best years of life in learning what procures for them neither bread nor respect. Surely we might, with advantage, have saved the cost of making these persons useless and miserable; surely, men may be brought up to be burdens to the public and objects of contempt to their neighbours at a somewhat smaller charge to the State. But such is our policy. We do not even stand neuter in the contest between truth and falsehood. We are not content to leave the natives to the influence of their hereditary prejudices. To the natural difficulties which obstruct the progress of sound science in the East we add fresh difficulties of our own making. Bounties and premiums, such as ought not to be given even for the propagation of truth, we lavish on false taste and false philosophy.

"By acting thus we create the very evil which we fear. We are making that opposition which we do not find. What we spend on the Arabic and Sanscrit colleges is not merely a dead loss to the cause of truth: it is the bounty-money paid to raise up champions of error. It goes to form a nest, not merely of helpless place-hunters, but of bigots prompted alike by passion and by interest to raise a cry against every useful scheme of education. If there should be any opposition among the natives to the change which I recommend, that opposition will be the effect of our own system. It will be headed by persons supported by our stipends and trained in our colleges. The longer we persevere in our present course, the more formidable will that opposition be. It will be every year re-inforced by recruits whom we are paying.

"From the native society left to itself we have no difficulties to apprehend; all the murmuring will come from that oriental interest which we have, by artificial means, called into being and nursed into strength.

"There is yet another fact, which is alone sufficient to prove that the feeling of the native public, when left to itself, is not such as the supporters of the old system represent it to be. The Committee have thought fit to lay out above a lac of rupees in printing Arabic and Sanscrit books. These books find no purchasers. It is very rarely that a single copy is disposed of. Twenty-three thousand volumes, most of them folios and quartos, fill the libraries, or rather the lumber-rooms, of this body. The Committee contrive to get rid of some portion of their vast stock of Oriental literature by giving books away. But they cannot give so fast as they print. About twenty thousand rupees a year are spent in adding fresh masses of waste paper to a hoard which, I should think, is already sufficiently ample. During the last three years, about sixty thousand rupees have been expended in this manner. The sale of Arabic and Sanscrit books, during those three years, has not yielded quite one thousand rupees. In the mean time the School-book Society is selling seven or eight thousand English volumes every year, and not only pays the expenses of printing, but realizes a profit of 20 per cent. on its outlay.

"The fact that the Hindoo law is to be learned chiefly from Sanscrit books, and the Mahomedan law from Arabic books, has been much insisted on, but seems not to bear at all on the question. We are commanded by Parliament to ascertain and digest the laws of India. The assistance of a law commission has been given to us for that purpose· As soon as the code is promulgated, the Shasters and the Hedeya will be useless to a Moonsiff or Sudder Ameen. I hope and trust that, before the boys who are now entering at the Madrassa and the Sanscrit college have completed their studies, this great work will be finished. It would be manifestly absurd to educate the rising generation with a view to a state of things which we mean to alter before they reach manhood.

"But there is yet another argument which seems even more untenable. It is said that the Sanscrit and Arabic are the languages in which the sacred books of a hundred millions of people are written, and that they are, on that account, entitled to peculiar encouragement. Assuredly it is the duty of the British Government in India to be not only tolerant, but neutral on all religious questions. But to encourage the study of a literature admitted to be of small intrinsic value only because that literature inculcates the most serious errors on the most important subjects, is a course hardly reconcilable with reason, with morality, or even with that very neutrality which ought, as we all agree, to be sacredly preserved. It is confessed that a language is barren of useful knowledge. We are told to teach it because it is fruitful of monstrous superstitions. We are to teach false history, false astronomy, false medicine, because we find them in company with a false religion. We abstain, and I trust shall always abstain, from giving any public encouragement to those who are engaged in the work of converting natives to Christianity. And, while we act thus, can we reasonably and decently bribe men out of the revenues of the state to waste their youth in learning how they are to purify themselves after touching an ass, or what text of the

Vedas they are to repeat to expiate the crime of killing a goat?

"It is taken for granted by the advocates of Oriental learning that no native of this country can possibly attain more than a mere smattering of English. They do not attempt to prove this; but they perpetually insinuate it. They designate the education which their opponents recommend as a mere spelling-book education. They assume it as undeniable, that the question is between a profound knowledge of Hindoo and Arabian literature and science on the one side, and a superficial knowledge of the rudiments of English on the other. This is not merely an assumption, but an assumption contrary to all reason and experience. We know that foreigners of all nations do learn our language sufficiently to have access to all the most abstruse knowledge which it contains, sufficiently to relish even the most delicate graces of our most idiomatic writers. There are in this very town natives who are quite competent to discuss political or scientific questions with fluency and precision in the English language. I have heard the very question on which I am now writing discussed by native gentlemen with a liberality and an intelligence which would do credit to any member of the Committee of Public Instruction. Indeed, it is unusual to find, even in the literary circles of the continent, any foreigner who can express himself in English with so much facility and correctness as we find in many Hindoos. Nobody, I suppose, will contend that English is so difficult to a Hindoo as Greek to an Englishman. Yet an intelligent English youth, in a much smaller number of years than our unfortunate pupils pass at the Sanscrit college, becomes able to read, to enjoy, and even to imitate, not unhappily, the composition of the best Greek authors. Less than half the time which enables an English youth to read Herodotus and Sophocles ought to enable a Hindoo to read Hume and Milton.

"To sum up what I have said: I think it clear that we are not fettered by the Act of Parliament of 1813; that we are not fettered by any pledge expressed or implied; that we are free to employ our funds as we choose; that we ought to employ them in teaching what is best worth knowing; that English is better worth knowing than Sanscrit or Arabic; that the natives are desirous to be taught English, and are not desirous to be taught Sanscrit or Arabic; that neither as the languages of law, nor as the languages of religion, have the Sanscrit and Arabic any peculiar claim to our encouragement; that it is possible to make natives of this country thoroughly good English scholars, and that to this end our efforts ought to be directed.

"In one point I fully agree with the gentlemen to whose general views I am opposed. I feel, with them, that it is impossible for us, with our limited means, to attempt to educate the body of the people. We must at present do our best to form a class who may be interpreters between us and the millions whom we govern; a class of persons, Indian in blood and colour, but English in taste, in opinions, in morals, and in intellect. To that class we may leave it to refine the vernacular dialects of the country, to enrich those dialects with terms of science borrowed from the Western nomenclature, and to render them by degrees fit vehicles for conveying knowledge to the great mass of the population.

"I would strictly respect all existing interests. I would deal even generously with all individuals who have had fair reason to expect a pecuniary provision. But I would strike at the root of the bad system which has hitherto been fostered by us. I would at once stop the printing of Arabic and Sanscrit books; I would abolish the Madrassa and the Sanscrit college at Calcutta. Benares is the great seat of Brahmanical learning; Delhi, of Arabic learning. If we retain the Sanscrit college at Benares and the Mahomedan college at Delhi, we do enough, and much more than enough in my opinion, for the Eastern languages. If the Benares and Delhi colleges should be retained, I would at least recommend that no stipend shall be given to any students who may hereafter repair thither, but that the people shall be left to make their own choice between the rival systems of education without being bribed by us to learn what they have no desire to know. The funds which would thus be placed at our disposal would enable us to give larger encouragement to the Hindoo college at Calcutta, and to establish in the principal cities throughout the Presidencies of Fort William and Agra schools in which the English language might be well and thoroughly taught.

"If the decision of his Lordship in Council should be such as I anticipate, I shall enter on the performance of my duties with the greatest zeal and alacrity. If, on the other hand, it be the opinion of the Government that the present system ought to remain unchanged, I beg that I may be permitted to retire from the chair of the Committee. I feel that I could not be of the smallest use there—I feel, also, that I should be lending my countenance to what I firmly believe to be a mere delusion. I believe that the present system tends, not to accelerate the progress of truth, but to delay the natural death of expiring error. I conceive that we have at present no right to the respectable name of a Board of Public Instruction. We are a Board for wasting public money, for printing books which are of less value than the paper on which they are printed was while it was blank; for giving artificial encouragement to absurd history, absurd metaphysics, absurd physics, absurd theology; for raising up a breed of scholars who find their scholarship an encumbrance and a blemish, who live on the public while they are receiving their education, and whose education is so utterly useless to them that, when they have received it, they must either starve or live on the public all the rest of their lives. Entertaining these opinions, I am naturally desirous to decline all share in the responsibility of a body which, unless it alters its whole mode of proceeding, I must consider not merely as useless, but as positively noxious."

THE END.

THE MUSSULMANS OF INDIA.

To the Editor of the Times.

SIR,—I have read with the utmost interest your very able articles on the learned letters of Colonel Nassau Lees and Sir Charles Trevelyan, on "Indian Mussulmans," but it seems to me the views of Colonel Nassau Lees have not been quite well understood. He does not advocate a return to the old policy; he does not desire the adoption of the study of Oriental classics to the exclusion of the English, but he says:—

"Have as much English as you like, but do not forcibly exclude the Oriental classical languages. Give the natives their choice between a thorough English education, with a little Arabic or Sanscrit, and a thorough Oriental education with a little English."

That appears to me rational and practicable, and, for my part, I should desire its realization.

I remain, honourable Sir,

Yours sincerely,

GARCIN DE TASSY,

Membre de l'Institut de France.

43, Rue St. André-des-Arts,
Paris, Nov. 17.